THE TRADING PLAYBOOK

MARKET BASICS AND PROVEN STRATEGIES FOR BEGINNERS

A Complete Guide to Understanding Financial Markets, Develeping Trading Skills, Managing Risk, and Building Long-Term Consistency

BY

MOHD ALFAIZ

FIRST EDITION

ACKNOWLEDGEMENTS

First and foremost, I want to express my sincere gratitude to you, the reader. Thank you for choosing this book and for taking the first step toward improving your knowledge and skills in trading. It truly means a lot to me.

I am deeply thankful to the incredible people who have supported and encouraged me throughout the writing of this book. To my family and friends—thank you for your unwavering belief in me, your patience, and your constant motivation.

I also extend my appreciation to my mentors, teachers, and everyone who has shared their knowledge, wisdom, and experiences that have shaped my understanding of the markets and trading.

Writing this book has been a journey of learning, reflection, and growth. My goal is to simplify complex concepts and provide practical insights that can help you build the right mindset, develop discipline, and trade with confidence.

Remember, the path to consistent success in trading is a marathon, not a sprint. Stay committed to learning, manage risk wisely, and keep improving every single day.

Thank you for choosing this book.
I hope it becomes a valuable companion on your trading journey.

INTRODUCTION

Welcome to ***The Trading Playbook***. Whether you are completely new to trading or just starting your journey, this book is for you.

The financial markets offer incredible opportunities, but they can also be unforgiving—especially for beginners. Most new traders fail not because they lack intelligence, but because they lack the right knowledge, preparation, and mindset. I wrote this book to help you avoid the common mistakes I made and countless others make, and to give you a clear roadmap to build a strong foundation before you risk your hard-earned money.

Inside this book, you will learn the core concepts of trading in simple and practical ways. We will start with the basics and gradually move into more advanced strategies, risk management techniques, and the psychology that separates consistent traders from the rest. Each chapter is designed to add a piece to your trading puzzle, helping you see the bigger picture over time.

This book is not about quick profits or shortcuts. It is about building knowledge, developing discipline, and creating a system you can trust. My goal is to equip you with the right tools, so you can trade with confidence, make better decisions, and grow consistently in the markets.

HOW TO USE THIS BOOK

I recommend reading this book from start to finish, in order. Take your time with each chapter, practice what you learn, and reflect on how you can apply it to your own trading journey. Don't rush the process—focus on understanding and implementing, not just reading.

Keep a notebook, test your strategies, learn from your results, and most importantly, stay disciplined. The markets will always be there, but your preparation today will determine your success tomorrow.

Trading is not about getting rich overnight. It is about developing the knowledge, discipline, and habits that lead to consistent long-term success. My hope is that this book becomes a trusted companion on your journey toward becoming a confident and disciplined trader.

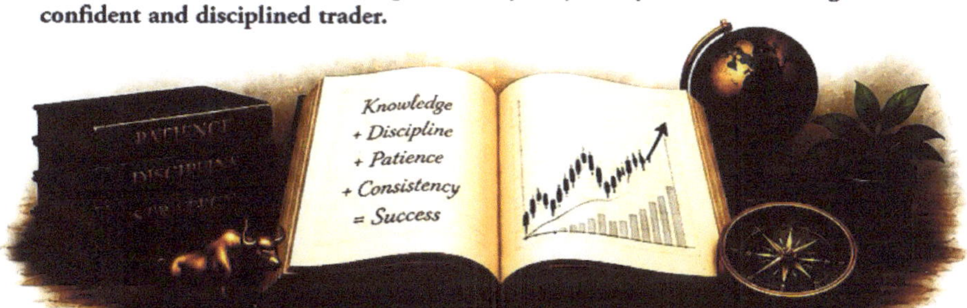

CONTENTS

CHAPTER 1

THE 10 STEPS TO START TRADING

INTRODUCTION

Many beginners enter the stock market with the expectation of making quick profits. However, successful trading requires knowledge, discipline, risk management, and continuous learning.

This chapter outlines the ten essential steps every aspiring trader should follow before placing their first trade.

STEP 1

OPEN A DEMAT AND TRADING ACCOUNT

The first requirement for participating in the stock market is opening a Demat account and a trading account with a registered broker.

A Demat account stores your securities in electronic form, while a trading account enables you to buy and sell financial instruments in the market.

Before selecting a broker, compare brokerage charges, platform features, customer support, and research tools.

STEP 2

CHOOSE YOUR TRADING STYLE

Different market participants have different objectives. Selecting the right trading style is crucial because it determines your strategy, time commitment, and risk exposure.

The most common styles include:

INTRADAY TRADING
Buying and selling securities within the same trading day.

SWING TRADING
Holding positions for several days or weeks to capture short-term market movements.

OPTIONS TRADING
Trading contracts that derive their value from underlying assets.

FUTURES TRADING
Trading standardized contracts that obligate the purchase or sale of an asset at a future date.

INVESTING
Building long-term wealth by holding quality assets for months or years.

STEP 3
LEARN THE FUNDAMENTALS

Once you have selected a trading style, focus on learning its principles and terminology.

Study how markets function, understand order types, learn market sessions, and familiarize yourself with the factors that influence price movement.

A strong foundation reduces costly mistakes later.

STEP 4

LEARN TO READ CHARTS AND CANDLESTICKS

Charts are one of the most important tools used by traders. Understanding candlestick charts helps you interpret market sentiment and identify potential opportunities.

Key concepts include:

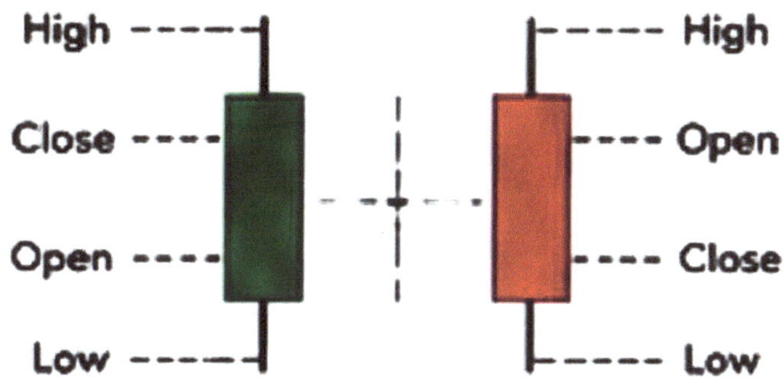

- Bullish and Bearish Candles
- Trend Analysis
- Chart Patterns
- Support and Resistance on Charts
- Volume Analysis

STEP 5

UNDERSTAND PRICE ACTION

Price action refers to analyzing raw market movement without relying heavily on indicators. It helps you understand what the market is actually doing.

Important concepts include:

- Support and Resistance
- Market Structure (Higher Highs, Lower Lows, etc.)
- Trend Identification
- Breakouts and Pullbacks
- Reversals

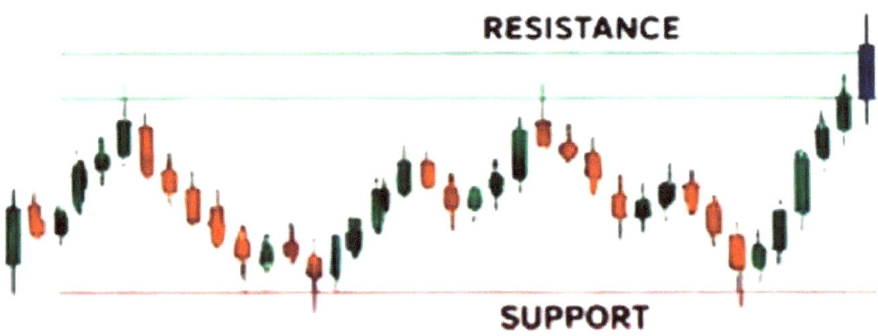

STEP 6
STUDY TECHNICAL INDICATORS

Technical indicators help traders analyze trends, momentum, volatility, and market conditions. They should be used to confirm price action, not to predict the market.

Common indicators include:

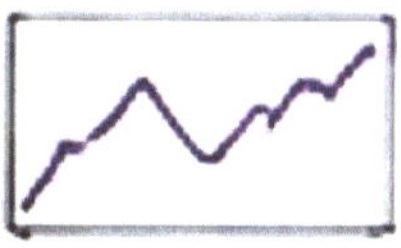

RSI (Relative Strength Index)
Measures the speed and change of price movements.

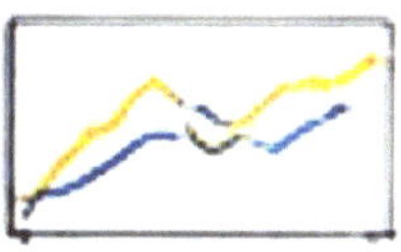

MA (Moving Average)
Helps identify the direction of the trend by smoothing price data.

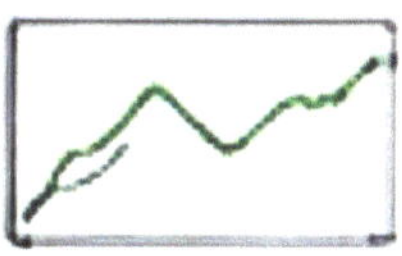

EMA (Exponential Moving Average)
Gives more weight to recent prices and reacts faster to market changes.

MACD (Moving Average Convergence Divergence)
Shows the relationship between two moving averages.

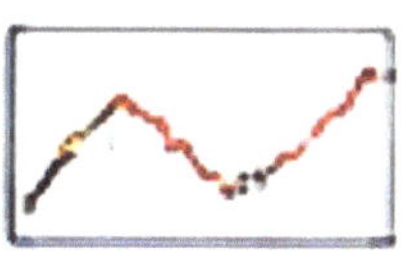

Supertrend
Helps identify the trend direction and potential reversal points.

STEP 7
LEARN RISK MANAGEMENT

Risk management is the most important skill for a trader. Protecting your capital ensures you stay in the game long enough to be profitable.

Key principles:

Use Stop Loss
Always define your maximum acceptable loss.

Risk Only a Small Percentage
Never risk more than 1–2% of your capital on a single trade.

Maintain Risk-Reward Ratio
Aim for trades where potential reward is greater than the risk.

Protect Your Capital
Capital preservation is more important than making profits.

STEP 8
DEVELOP A TRADING STRATEGY

A trading strategy defines your entry, exit, and risk management rules. It removes emotions and brings consistency to your trading.

A good strategy includes:

- ✓ Entry Criteria: When to enter a trade
- ✓ Exit Criteria: When to exit a trade
- ✓ Stop Loss Rules: Where to place stop loss
- ✓ Take Profit Rules: Where to book profits
- ✓ Position Sizing: How much capital to risk
- ✓ Risk-Reward Ratio: Minimum R:R for valid trades

Remember:
A strategy should be simple, testable, and aligned with your trading style.

STEP 9
BACKTEST AND PRACTICE

Before trading with real money, test your strategy using historical data. This helps you understand its strengths, weaknesses, and probability.

BACKTEST YOUR STRATEGY

Use past market data to see how your strategy would have performed.

PRACTICE WITH PAPER TRADING

Trade in a simulated environment without risking real money. It builds confidence and helps you refine your approach.

Goal: Build consistency before you risk real capital.

STEP 10

START TRADING WITH DISCIPLINE

After gaining knowledge, testing your strategy, and managing risk effectively, you are ready to start trading with real money.

Success comes from discipline:

- **Follow Your Plan:** Stick to your trading rules.
- **Control Emotions:** Avoid fear and greed.
- **Review and Improve:** Learn from every trade.
- **Stay Patient and Consistent:** Results take time.

DISCIPLINE TODAY, FREEDOM TOMORROW.

FINAL THOUGHT

These ten steps form the foundation of a successful trading journey. Focus on learning, practicing, and improving every day.

> "The market is a device for transferring money from the impatient to the patient."
>
> — *Warren Buffett*

CHAPTER 2

UNDERSTANDING FINANCIAL MARKETS

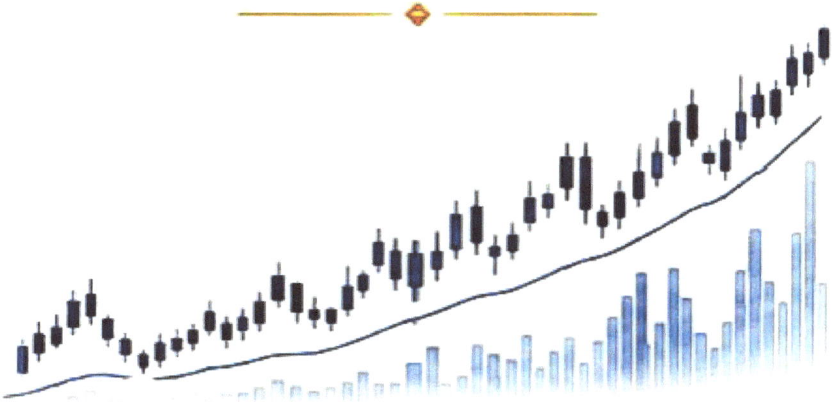

Before a trader can analyze charts or develop strategies, it is essential to understand the environment in which trading takes place. Financial markets connect buyers and sellers, allowing the exchange of financial assets and helping determine prices through supply and demand.

In this chapter, you will learn about the different types of financial markets, the participants who influence them, and the factors that drive price movements. A strong understanding of these concepts will help you build a solid foundation for your trading journey.

2.1 WHAT IS A FINANCIAL MARKET?

A financial market is a marketplace where buyers and sellers trade financial assets such as stocks, bonds, commodities, currencies, and derivatives.

Just as a vegetable market brings together buyers and sellers of vegetables, a financial market brings together buyers and sellers of financial instruments.

Financial markets play a vital role in the economy by:

Facilitating the buying and selling of assets	Providing liquidity to investors	Helping businesses raise capital	Supporting economic growth	Determining fair prices through supply and demand

Without financial markets, businesses would struggle to obtain funding, and investors would have limited opportunities to grow their wealth.

2.2 TYPES OF FINANCIAL MARKETS

Financial markets can be divided into several categories, each serving a specific purpose.

1. STOCK MARKET

The stock market allows investors to buy and sell shares of publicly listed companies. When you purchase a company's stock, you become a partial owner of that business.

Examples: Reliance Industries, TCS, Infosys, HDFC Bank

2. COMMODITY MARKET

Commodity markets facilitate the trading of physical goods and raw materials.

Examples: Gold, Silver, Crude Oil, Natural Gas, Agricultural Products

3. FOREIGN EXCHANGE (FOREX) MARKET

The Forex market is the largest financial market in the world. It involves the buying and selling of currencies.

Examples: USD/INR, EUR/USD, GBP/USD, USD/JPY

4. CRYPTOCURRENCY MARKET

The cryptocuurency market consists of digital assets that operate on blockchain technology.

Examples: Bitcoin (BTC), Ethereum (ETH), Solana (SOL)

5. BOND MARKET

The bond market allows governments and corporations to borrow money from investors.

When an investor buys a bond, they are essentially lending money in exchange for periodic interest payments.

2.3 WHY DO MARKET PRICES CHANGE?

One of the most common questions asked by beginners is:

> "Why does the market move up and down?"

The answer lies in supply and demand.

When demand exceeds supply, prices rise.

When supply exceeds demand, prices fall.

Several factors influence supply and demand:

Economic News

Interest rates, inflation data, GDP growth, and employment reports can significantly impact prices.

Company Performance

Strong earnings reports often push prices higher, while weak results can lead to declines.

Market Sentiment

Investor emotions such as fear and greed frequently influence market behavior.

Global Events

Wars, elections, natural disasters, and policy changes can create volatility in markets.

News & Media

News headlines [illegible] [illegible] media reports can trigger rapid price moves.

2.4 BULL MARKETS VS BEAR MARKETS

Markets move in cycles. Understanding market trends helps you adapt your trading strategy to different conditions.

BULL MARKET

A bull market is a period during which prices are generally rising

Characteristics include:

- Strong investor confidence
- Economic growth
- Increasing stock prices
- Positive market sentiment

Bull markets create opportunities for long-term investors and trend-following traders.

BEAR MARKET

A bear market is a period during which prices are generally falling

Characteristics include:

- Weak investor confidence
- Economic uncertainty
- Declining stock prices
- Negative market sentiment

Bear markets often test a trader's discipline and risk management skills.

2.5 KEY MARKET PARTICIPANTS

Financial markets consist of different participants, each playing a unique role.

1. RETAIL TRADERS

Individual traders who buy and sell assets using their own capital.

2. INSTITUTIONAL INVESTORS

Large organizations such as mutual funds, hedge funds, insurance companies, and pension funds that invest huge amounts of money.

3. BANKS

Financial institutions that provide liquidity, facilitate transactions, and offer various financial services.

4. MARKET MAKERS

Entities that continuously quote buy and sell prices to improve market liquidity and ensure smooth trading.

5. GOVERNMENTS & CENTRAL BANKS

Organizations that influence markets through fiscal and monetary policies, interest rates, and regulations.

2.6 IMPORTANT MARKET TERMS

Before progressing further, every trader should understand the following terms:

LIQUIDITY	The ease with which an asset can be bought or sold without significantly affecting its price.
VOLATILITY	The degree of price fluctuation in a market.
VOLUME	The total number of shares or contracts traded during a specific period.
BID PRICE	The highest price a buyer is willing to pay.
ASK PRICE	The lowest price a seller is willing to accept.
SPREAD	The difference between the bid price and the ask price.

FINAL THOUGHT

Understanding financial markets is the foundation of every successful trading journey. Throughout this chapter, we explored the structure of markets, the key participants, and the factors that influence price movements.

Knowledge gives you clarity, but discipline turns that knowledge into consistent results. Stay curious, keep learning, and always remember that the markets will reward those who are patient and prepared.

> **An investment in knowledge pays the best interest.**
>
> — Benjamin Franklin

CHAPTER 3

CANDLESTICK CHARTS AND MARKET STRUCTURE

INTRODUCTION

Candlestick charts are one of the most powerful tools used by traders to analyze price movements. They provide a visual representation of market activity and help traders understand the battle between buyers and sellers.

Every candlestick contains important information about price action during a specific period. By learning how to read candlesticks, traders can identify trends, reversals, and potential trading opportunities.

In this chapter, you will learn the anatomy of a candlestick, important candlestick patterns, and how market structure helps traders understand the overall direction of the market.

Mastering these concepts will provide a strong foundation for technical analysis and improve your decision-making as a trader.

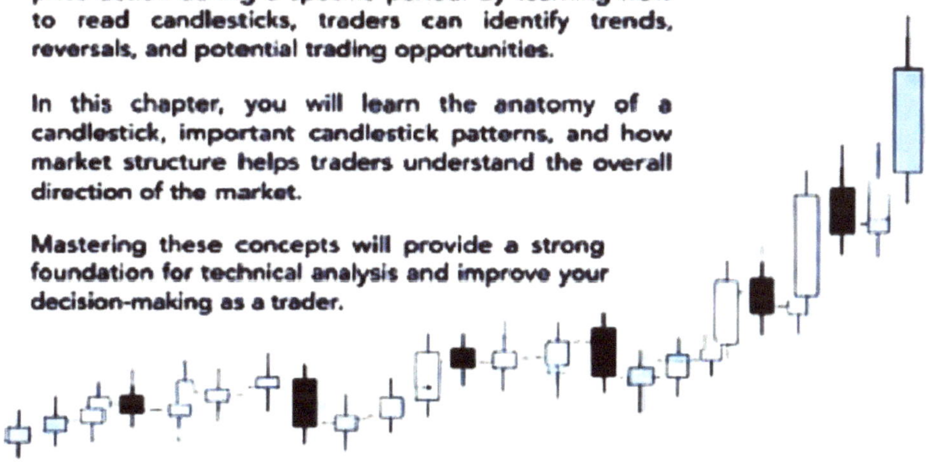

ANATOMY OF A CANDLESTICK

A candlestick represents the price movement of an asset during a specific period.

Each candlestick consists of four important components:

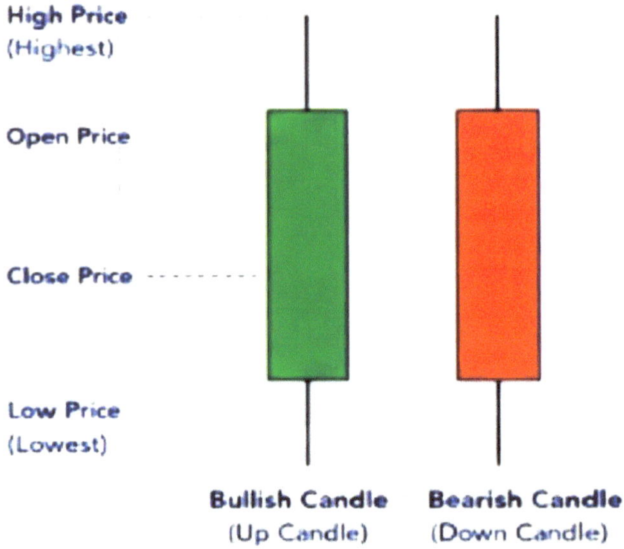

- **High Price**
  The highest price reached during the period
- **Open Price**
  The price at which the period begins
- **Close Price**
  The price at which the period ends.
- **Low Price**
  The lowest price reached during the period

Bullish Candle:

A bullish candle forms when the closing price is higher than the opening price. It indicates buying pressure and positive market sentiment.

Bearish Candle:

A bearish candle forms when the closing price is lower than the opening price. It indicates selling pressure and negative market sentiment.

BULLISH AND BEARISH CANDLES

Candlesticks reveal the ongoing battle between buyers and sellers. The color of the candle body shows who is in control.

BULLISH CANDLE (GREEN)

- Close price is higher than open price.
- Buyers are in control.
- Shows strength and upward momentum.

More green candles in a trend indicate strong buying pressure.

BEARISH CANDLE (RED)

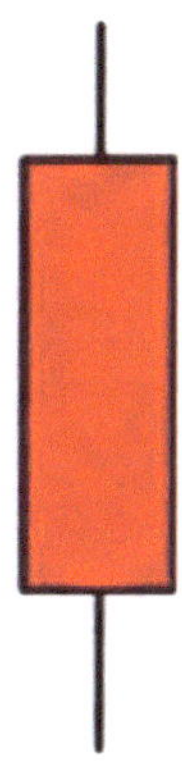

- Close price is lower than open price.
- Sellers are in control.
- Shows weakness and downward momentum.

More red candles in a trend indicate strong selling pressure.

MARUBOZU CANDLES

Marubozu candles show strong momentum in one direction. They have no wicks (shadows) on either side.

BULLISH MARUBOZU

- Long green body
- No upper wick
- No lower wick
- Buyers controlled the entire session
- Strong bullish momentum

BEARISH MARUBOZU

- Long red body
- No upper wick
- No lower wick
- Sellers controlled the entire session
- Strong bearish momentum

A Bullish Marubozu shows strong buying pressure with no rejection from sellers.

A Bearish Marubozu shows strong selling pressure with no rejection from buyers.

DOJI CANDLESTICK

A Doji candlestick forms when the opening and closing prices are almost equal.

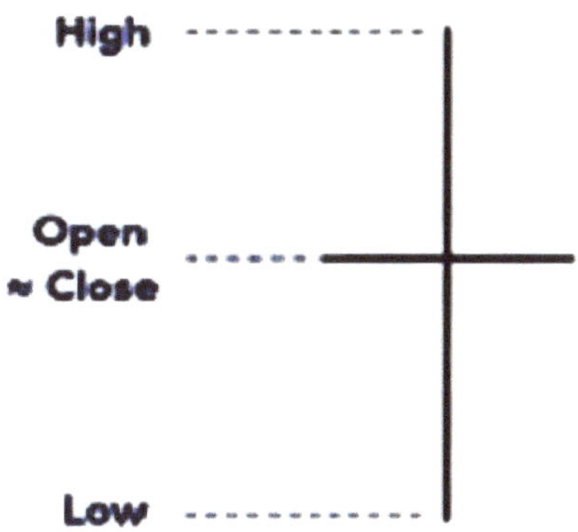

- Shows indecision in the market.
- Buyers and sellers are in balance.
- Often signals a potential reversal when it appears at key levels.

Key Point

A Doji by itself is not a strong signal. It becomes more reliable when confirmed by the next candle or by other factors like support and resistance.

HAMMER AND INVERTED HAMMER

HAMMER (BULLISH REVERSAL)

- Small body at the top with a long lower wick.
- Forms at the bottom of a downtrend.
- Signals potential bullish reversal.

The long lower wick shows that sellers tried to push prices down, but buyers took control and pushed prices up before the close.

INVERTED HAMMER (BULLISH REVERSAL)

- Small body at the bottom with a long upper wick.
- Forms at the bottom of a downtrend.
- Signals potential bullish reversal.

The long upper wick shows that buyers tried to push prices up, but sellers took control and pushed prices down before the close.

SHOOTING STAR AND HANGING MAN

SHOOTING STAR (BEARISH REVERSAL)

- Small body at the bottom with a long upper wick.
- Forms at the top of an uptrend.
- Signals potential bearish reversal.

HANGING MAN (BEARISH REVERSAL)

- Small body at the top with a long lower wick.
- Forms at the top of an uptrend.
- Signals potential bearish reversal.

MARKET STRUCTURE BASICS

Market structure helps us understand the direction and strength of a trend. There are four key components:

HIGHER HIGHS (HH)

Price makes a new high that is higher than the previous high.

HIGHER LOWS (HL)

Price makes a new low that is higher than the previous low.

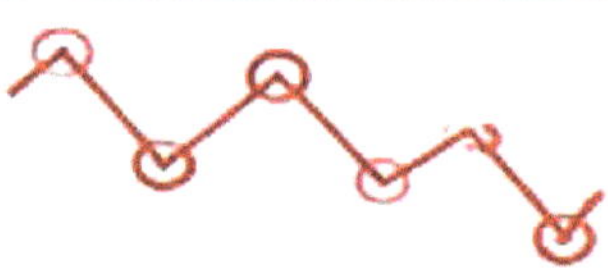

LOWER HIGHS (LH)

Price makes a new high that is lower than the previous high.

LOWER LOWS (LL)

Price makes a new low that is lower than the previous low.

UPTREND AND DOWNTREND

UPTREND (BULLISH STRUCTURE)

- Consists of higher highs and higher lows.
- Indicates buying pressure and strength.
- Traders look for buying opportunities in an uptrend.

DOWNTREND (BEARISH STRUCTURE)

- Consists of lower highs and lower lows.
- Indicates selling pressure and weakness.
- Traders look for selling opportunities in a downtrend.

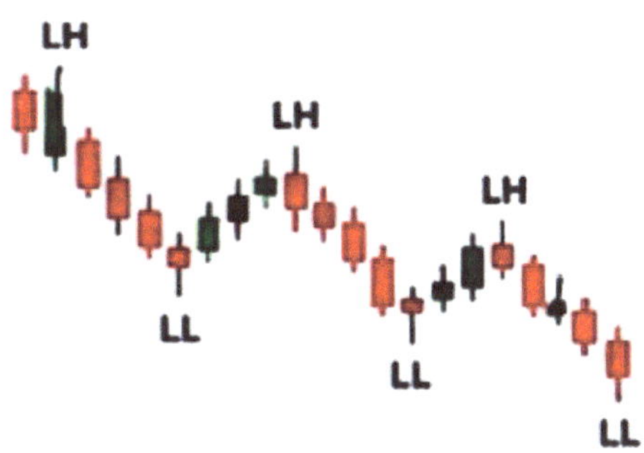

SIDEWAYS MARKET AND CONSOLIDATION

A sideways market (or consolidation) occurs when price moves within a horizontal range.

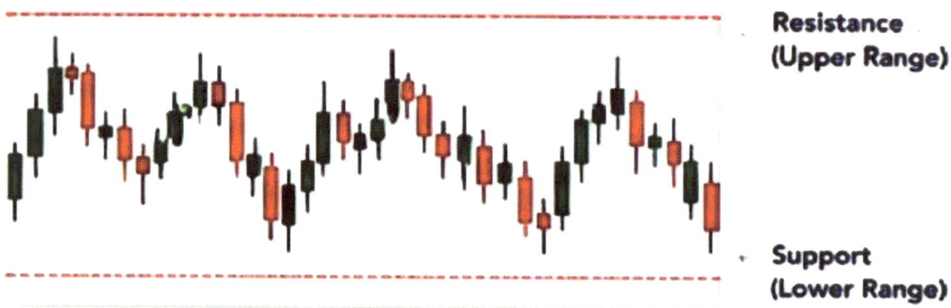

- There is no clear direction.
- Price moves between support and resistance.
- Breakouts can create strong moves in either direction.

In sideways markets, traders can buy near support and sell near resistance, or wait for a breakout with confirmation.

CHAPTER SUMMARY

In this chapter, we covered the essential building blocks of candlestick charts and market structure.

- We learned the anatomy of a candlestick and the meaning of open, high, low, and close.
- We studied important candlestick types: bullish, bearish, doji, marubozu, hammer, inverted hammer, shooting star, and hanging man.
- We learned how these patterns help identify potential reversals and market sentiment.
- We understood market structure: higher highs, higher lows, lower highs, and lower lows.
- We explored trends: uptrend, downtrend, and sideways market, and how they guide trading decisions.
- Mastering these concepts helps traders read the market better and make more informed trading decisions.

FINAL THOUGHT

Candlestick patterns and market structure are like a language that the market speaks every day.

The more you learn this language, the better you will understand price action and the more confident you will become.

Remember, successful trading is not about predicting the future — it is about preparing for it.

> **Discipline is doing what needs to be done, even when you don't feel like doing it.**
>
> **— Mark Douglas**

CHAPTER 4

PRICE ACTION TRADING

The Purest Form of Market Analysis

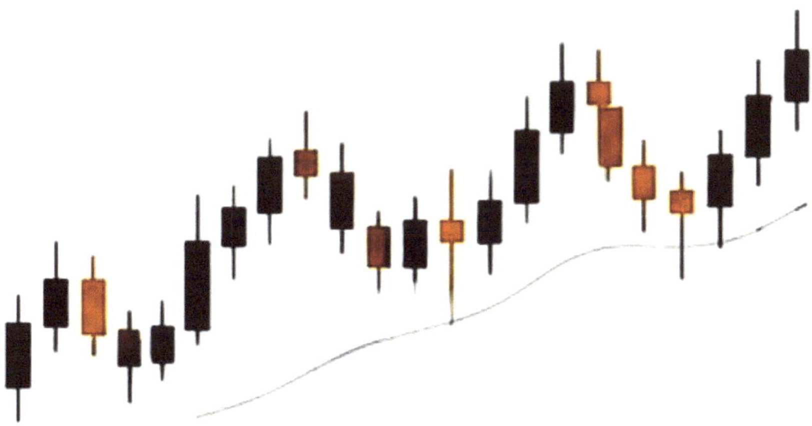

Price action trading is the art of reading the market using only price and volume—without relying on indicators. It helps you understand what buyers and sellers are doing right now, so you can make high-probability trading decisions.

WHAT IS PRICE ACTION?

Price action is the movement of price over time. It reflects the collective behavior of all market participants.

Every candlestick tells a story—of buying and selling, fear and greed, momentum and exhaustion.

When you learn to read price action, you see the market as it really is, without any lag or distortion.

> The goal is not to predict the market,
> but to read it.

WHY PRICE ACTION WORKS

- **Real-Time**
  It shows you what is happening right now, not what happened in the past.
- **Universal**
  It works in all markets—Forex, Stocks, Crypto, Commodities. All you need is price.
- **Simple and Clear**
  No lagging indicators. Just raw price movement.
- **Based on Supply and Demand**
  Price action is the direct result of buyers and sellers interacting in the market.
- **Repeatable**
  Market behavior repeats because human behavior doesn't change.

THE LANGUAGE OF CANDLESTICKS

Candlesticks are the foundation of price action trading.
Each candle shows four key prices within a specific time period.

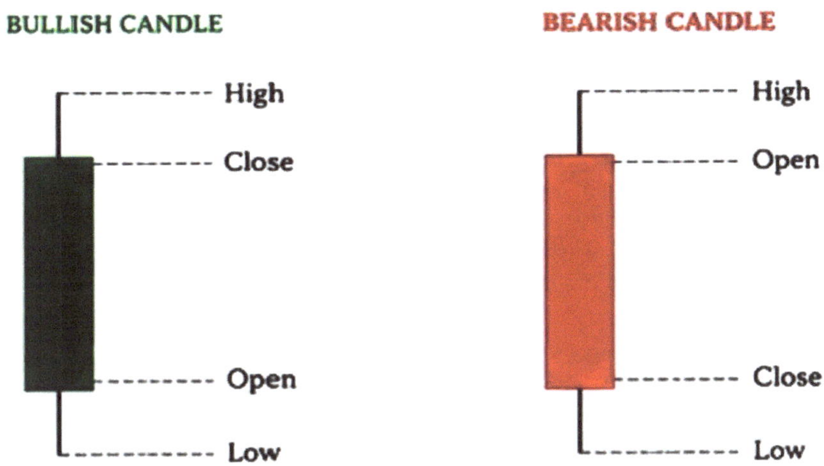

The relationship between these four prices gives us valuable information about market sentiment and strength.

SUPPORT AND RESISTANCE

Support is a price level where buyers are strong enough to prevent the price from falling further.

Resistance is a price level where sellers are strong enough to prevent the price from rising further.

★ KEY POINTS

- Price respects support and resistance.
- The more times a level is tested, the stronger it becomes.
- When price breaks a level, that level often becomes the opposite (support becomes resistance and vice versa).

PRICE ACTION PATTERNS

Certain patterns form repeatedly on charts. Here are the most important ones every trader should know.

1. DOUBLE TOP (BEARISH)

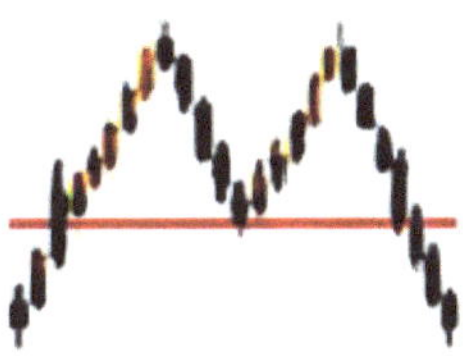

Forms two peaks at the same level. Breaks below the neckline. Indicates a potential downtrend.

2. DOUBLE BOTTOM (BULLISH)

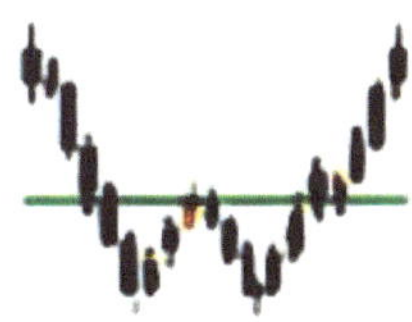

Forms two bottoms at the same level. Breaks above the neckline. Indicates a potential uptrend.

3. HEAD AND SHOULDERS (BEARISH)

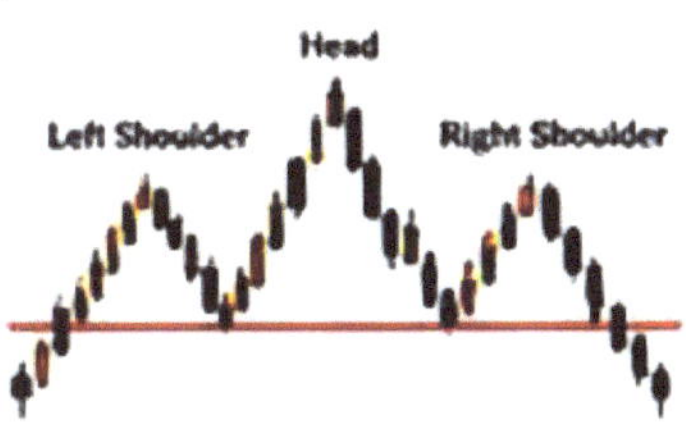

Forms a head between two shoulders.
Breaks below the neckline.
Strong bearish reversal pattern.

4. INVERSE HEAD AND SHOULDERS (BULLISH)

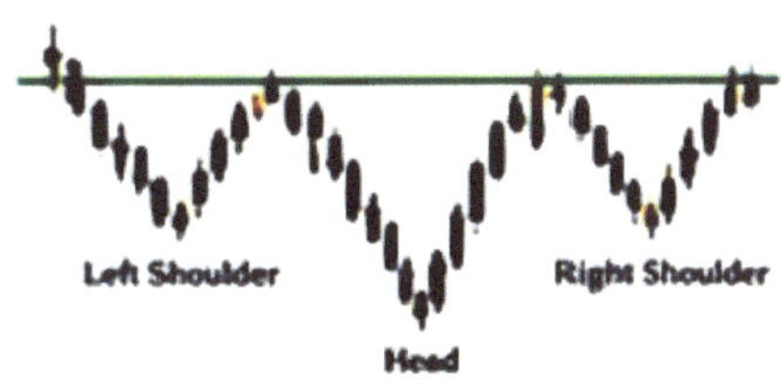

Forms an inverse head and shoulders.
Breaks above the neckline.
Strong bullish reversal pattern.

HOW TO TRADE PRICE ACTION

TREND CONTINUATION (BREAKOUT)

1. Identify a strong level.
2. Wait for price to break the level with a strong candle.
3. Enter on retest or breakout.
4. Place stop below the level.
5. Let profit run.

TREND REVERSAL (REVERSAL)

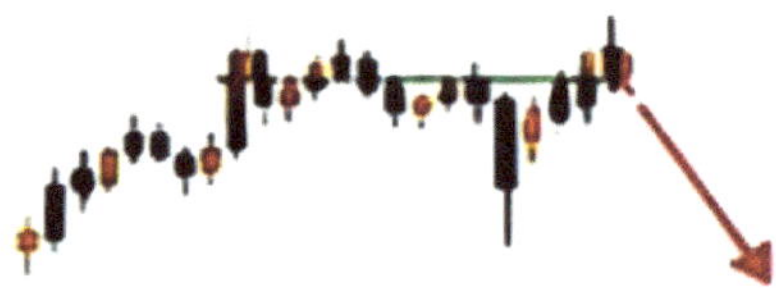

1. Identify a key support/resistance.
2. Look for rejection candles (e.g., Pin Bar, Engulfing).
3. Enter in the opposite direction.
4. Place stop above/below the level.
5. Target the next key level.

REMEMBER

Price action is not about prediction.
It is about reading the market and reacting to it.
Let price show you the way.

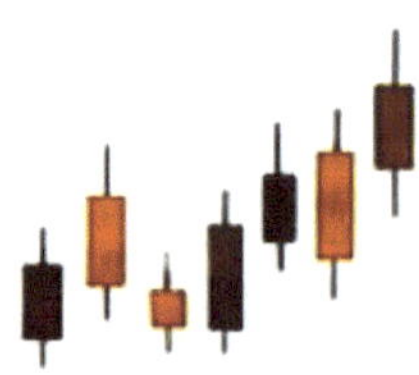

BREAKOUTS AND RETESTS

A breakout occurs when price moves above a key resistance level (in an uptrend) or below a key support level (in a downtrend) with strong momentun.

After the breakout, price often returns to retest that level. If the level holds, the trend is likely to continue.

BULLISH BREAKOUT EXAMPLE

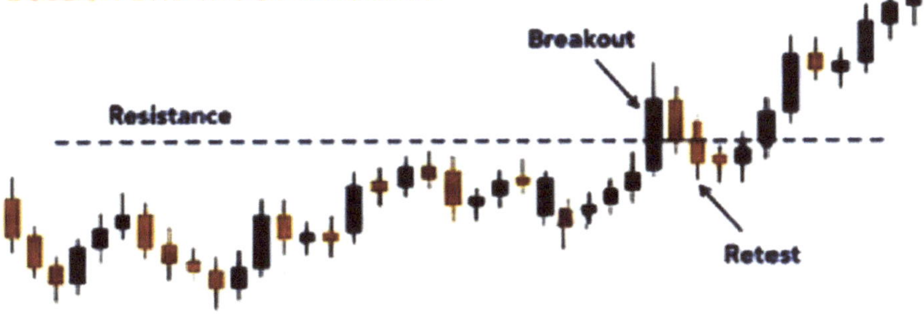

BEARISH BREAKOUT EXAMPLE

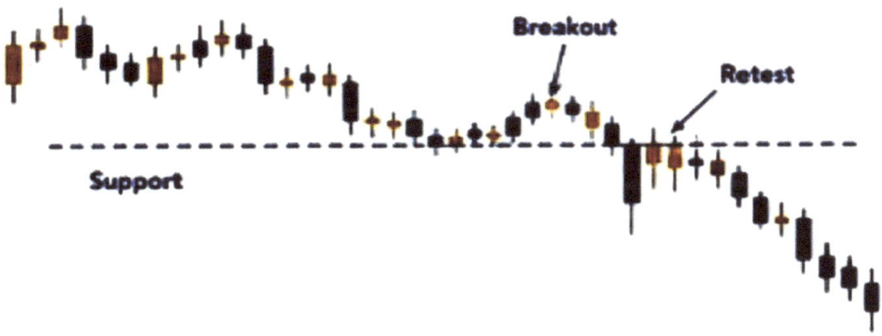

TRADING WITH CONFLUENCE

Confluence means combining multiple factors that increase the probability of a successful trade.

When price action aligns with other factors, your trades become stronger and more reliable.

Examples of confluence:

- Support / Resistance levels
- Trend direction
- Chart patterns
- Moving averages
- Volume

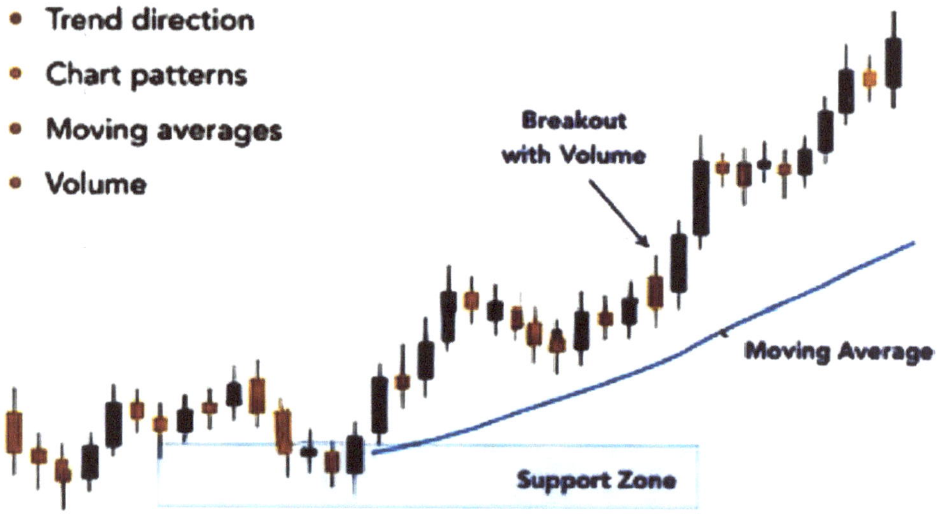

The more confluence your setup has, the higher the probability of success.

COMMON PRICE ACTION MISTAKES

Avoiding mistakes is just as important as finding good setups.

✗ Chasing candles

Entering late after a big move increases risk. Wait for proper setups.

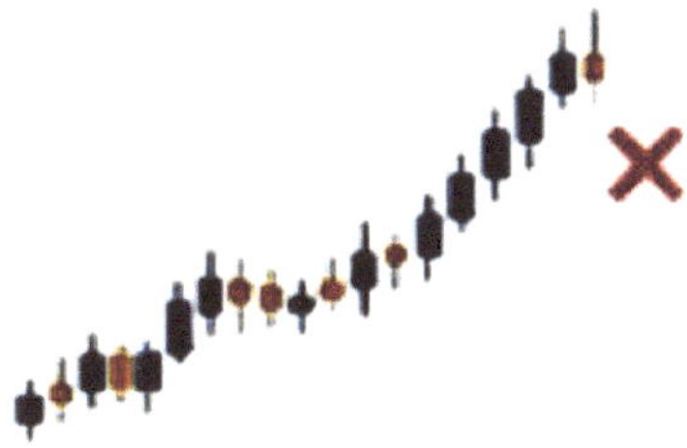

✗ Trading against the trend

Fighting the trend lowers your probability of success.

✗ Ignoring market structure

Not understanding support, resistance, and structure leads to poor decisions.

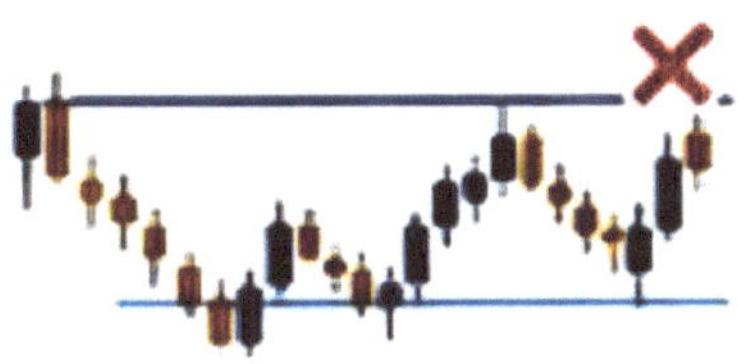

✗ Overtrading

Too many trades lead to mistakes and unnecessary losses. Quality over quantity.

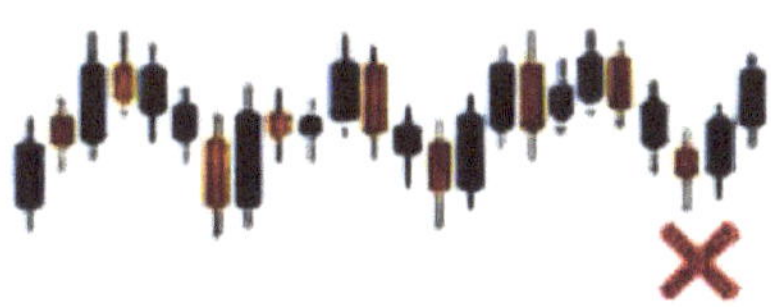

CHAPTER SUMMARY

In this chapter, you learned:

- What breakout and retest are and how they create high-probability setups.
- How to combine multiple factors (confluence) like trend, support/resistance, candlesticks, moving averages, and volume for stronger trades.
- Common price action mistakes that can hurt your performance and how to avoid them.
- The importance of market structure in identifying good trading opportunities.
- How to trade price action with discipline, patience, and a clear plan.

FINAL THOUGHT

Price action is not about guessing
what will happen next.
It's about reading what is happening now
and reacting with a plan.

The market is always speaking.
The more you practice, the better you will understand its language.
Stay patient, stay consistent, and let price action
be your guide to success.

CHAPTER 5

SUPPORT AND RESISTANCE

The Foundation of Market Structure

Support and resistance are key levels where price tends to stop, reverse, or react. Understanding these levels helps you identify high-probability trading opportunities and make better decisions.

INTRODUCTION

Support and resistance are among the most important concepts in technical analysis.

These price levels help traders understand where the market may pause, reverse, or continue its movement.

Support acts as a floor where buying pressure tends to prevent prices from falling further.

Resistance acts as a ceiling where selling pressure often prevents prices from moving higher.

By learning how to identify these levels, traders can improve their entries, exits, stop-loss placement, and profit targets.

In this chapter, you will learn how support and resistance levels are formed, how to draw them correctly, and how to use them in real trading situations.

WHAT IS SUPPORT?

Support is a price level where a downtrend or pullback tends to pause due to buying interest.

At support, buyers step in and prevent the price from falling further.

This creates a floor that holds the price and often leads to a bounce.

The more times price touches a level and holds, the stronger the support.

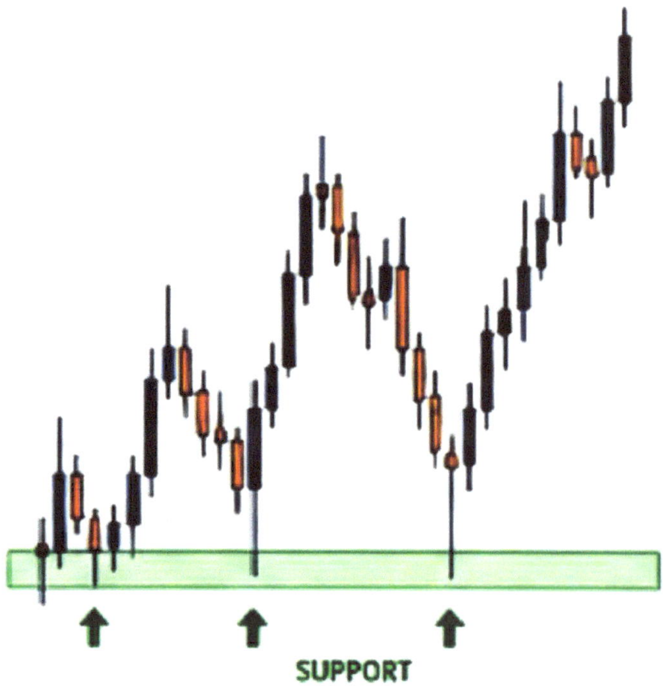

WHAT IS RESISTANCE?

Resistance is a price level where an uptrend or rally tends to pause due to selling pressure.

At resistance, sellers step in and prevent the price from moving higher.

This creates a ceiling that holds the price and often leads to a pullback.

The more times price touches a level and rejects, the stronger the resistance.

ROLE REVERSAL

When price breaks through a support or resistance level and holds, that level often becomes its opposite.

Support that is broken can turn into resistance.

Resistance that is broken can turn into support.

This is called role reversal, and it is a powerful concept in trading.

How to Draw Levels

To draw strong support and resistance levels:

- Identify swing highs and swing lows
- Draw horizontal lines across those key points.
- Focus on areas where price has reacted multiple times in the past.
- Keep the lines clean and avoid overcrowding the chart.

Common Mistakes

Even simple concepts like support and resistance can be misunderstood.

Avoiding these common mistakes can save you from costly trading decisions.

- **Drawing Too Many Levels**
  Cluttering your chart makes it hard to focus on the most important levels.
- **Ignoring Higher Time Frames**
  Lower time frame levels are less reliable. Always check the bigger picture.
- **Expecting Exact Bounces**
  Price may react before or after the level. Look for confirmation.
- **Forgetting Role Reversal**
  A level that worked before can switch role. Always be prepared for the opposite reaction.
- **Not Considering Context**
  News, trend, and momentum all affect how levels behave.

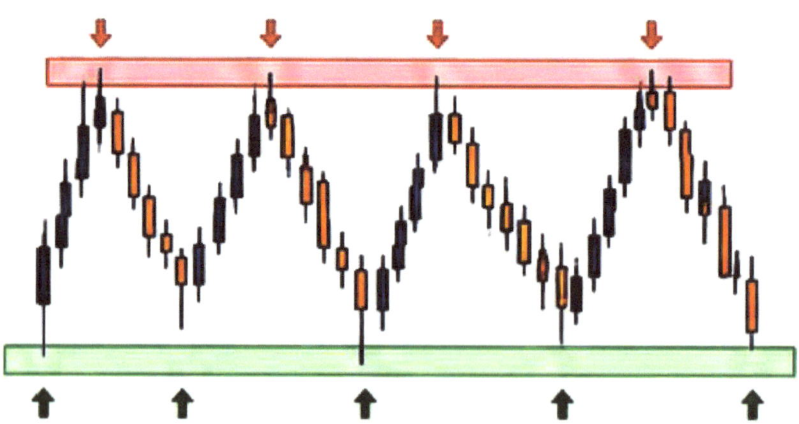

Using Support and Resistance in Trading

Support and resistance levels can be used in many ways to improve your trading.

Here are the most common applications:

- **Entries**
  Buy near support and sell near resistance with confirmation.
- **Stop-Loss Placement**
  Place stops beyond the level to avoid being stopped out by normal price swings.
- **Take-Profit Targets**
  Use the next support or resistance level as your profit target.
- **Breakout Trading**
  When price breaks a strong level, trade in the direction of the breakout with confirmation.
- **Confluence**
  Stronger levels form where support/ resistance aligns with trendlines, moving averages, or chart patterns.

Chapter Summary

Support and resistance are the foundation of technical analysis.

They help you understand market structure and make high-probability trading decisions.

Key takeaways from this chapter:

- Support is a price level where buying pressure prevents the price from falling further.
- Resistance is a price level where selling pressure prevents the price from rising further.
- These levels are formed by past price actions and market psychology.
- When a level breaks, it can turn into the opposite level (role reversal).
- Strong levels are the ones that have been tested multiple times.
- Use support and resistance for entries, exits, stop-loss placement, and profit targets.

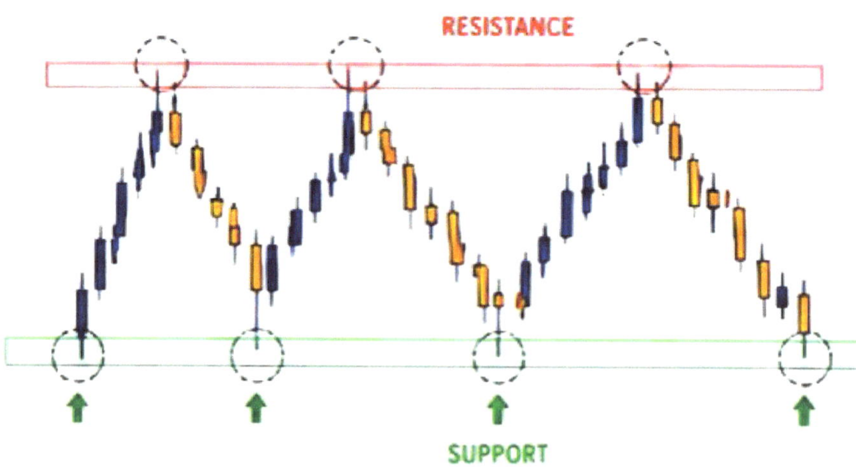

FINAL THOUGHT

Support and resistance levels will always be part of the market.

The more you study them, the better you will understand price behavior.

Be patient, practice often, and let the market show you how powerful these levels can be in your trading journey.

"

The market respects levels that traders respect.

CHAPTER 6

TECHNICAL INDICATORS

Tools That Help Traders Read the Market

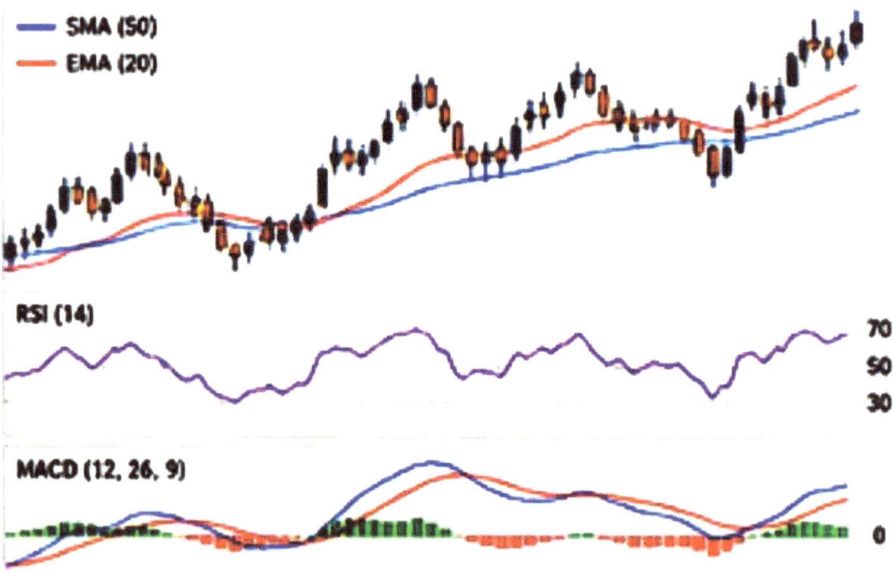

Technical indicators are mathematical calculations based on price, volume, or open interest. They help traders identify trends, momentum, and potential reversals to make better trading decisions.

WHAT ARE TECHNICAL INDICATORS?

Technical indicators are tools used to analyze price data and market activity.

They are based on mathematical formulas and are plotted on charts to help traders identify patterns, trends, and potential entry or exit points.

WHY TRADERS USE THEM

- Identify trends
- Measure momentum
- Spot overbought or oversold conditions
- Confirm price action
- Improve timing

ADVANTAGES

- Help simplify market data
- Provide objective signals
- Work in all markets

LIMITATIONS

- Lagging by nature
- Can give false signals
- Should not be used alone

Moving Averages (SMA & EMA)

Moving averages smooth out price data to identify the direction of the trend.

SMA (Simple Moving Average) gives equal weight to all prices.

EMA (Exponential Moving Average) gives more weight to recent prices, making it more responsive.

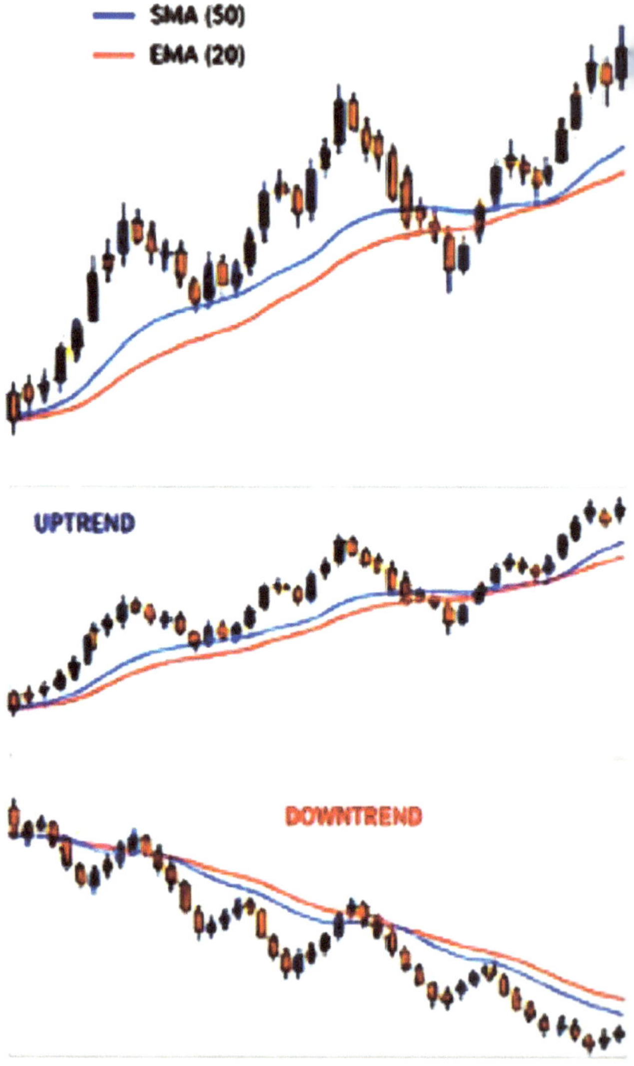

HOW THEY HELP

- Identify trend direction
- Act as dynamic support or resistance
- Help with entry and exit timing

Relative Strength Index (RSI)

RSI is a momentum indicator that measures the speed and change of price movements.

It moves between 0 and 100.

RSI helps identify overbought and oversold conditions in the market.

KEY LEVELS

- Above 70: Overbought
- Below 30: Oversold
- 50: Neutral level

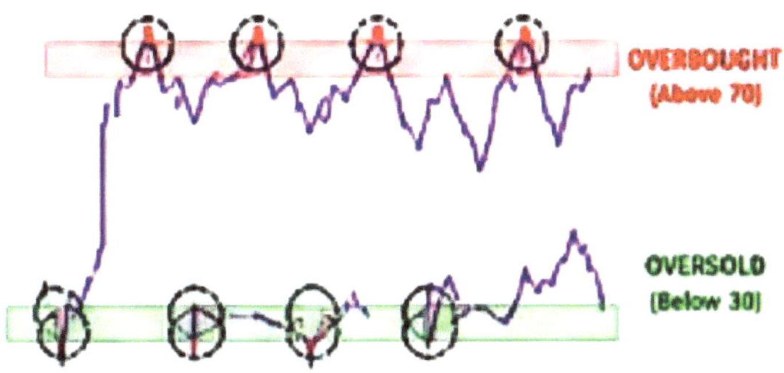

MACD (Moving Average Convergence Divergence)

MACD shows the relationship between two moving averages of a security's price.

It consists of three components:

- **MACD Line** (typically 12 EMA minus 26 EMA)
- **Signal Line** (9 EMA of the MACD Line)
- **Histogram** (The difference between MACD Line and Signal Line)

MACD helps traders identify trend direction, momentum, and potential reversals.

COMBINING INDICATORS

Using multiple indicators together increases the probability of making better trading decisions.

Combining indicators helps confirm signals and reduces the chance of false signals.

EXAMPLE SETUP

- Trend: Moving Average
- Momentum: RSI
- Confirmation: MACD
- Price Action: Support and Resistance

KEY TAKEAWAY

When all indicators agree, the signal becomes stronger.

COMMON MISTAKES

Even the best tools can hurt your trading if used the wrong way.

Avoid these common mistakes to get the best results.

- **Using Too Many Indicators**
  Adding too many indicators creates confusion and sends mixed signals.
- **Indicator Overload**
  Too many indicators on your chart can lead to analysis paralysis and poor timing.
- **Ignoring Price Action**
  Indicators confirm what price is doing. Never ignore the price movement.
- **Blindly Following Signals**
  Indicators are not 100% accurate. Always use proper risk management and wait for confirmation.

USING INDICATORS EFFECTIVELY

Indicators are most effective when used the right way.

Here's how to use them to improve your trading.

- **Indicators as Confirmation Tools**
  Use indicators to confirm what price action is already showing.

- **Combine Indicators with Price Action**
  The best results come when indicators support key levels and patterns.

- **Risk Management Comes First**
  No indicator is 100% accurate. Always use stop-losses and proper position sizing.

- **Practical Trading Example**
  In an uptrend, price is above the 50 EMA, RSI is above 50, and MACD is positive. Wait for a pullback to support, then look for a long entry.

CHAPTER SUMMARY

Technical indicators are powerful tools that help traders analyze the market and make better decisions.

Key takeaways from this chapter:

- **Technical Indicators**
  Tools based on mathematical calculations that help analyze price, momentum, and market conditions.
- **Moving Averages (SMA & EMA)**
  Help identify the direction of the trend and act as dynamic support or resistance.
- **Relative Strength Index (RSI)**
  Measures momentum and helps identify overbought and oversold conditions.
- **MACD (Moving Average Convergence Divergence)**
  Shows the relationship between moving averages and helps identify momentum and trend changes.
- **Combining Indicators**
  Using multiple indicators together with price action improves accuracy and reduces false signals.

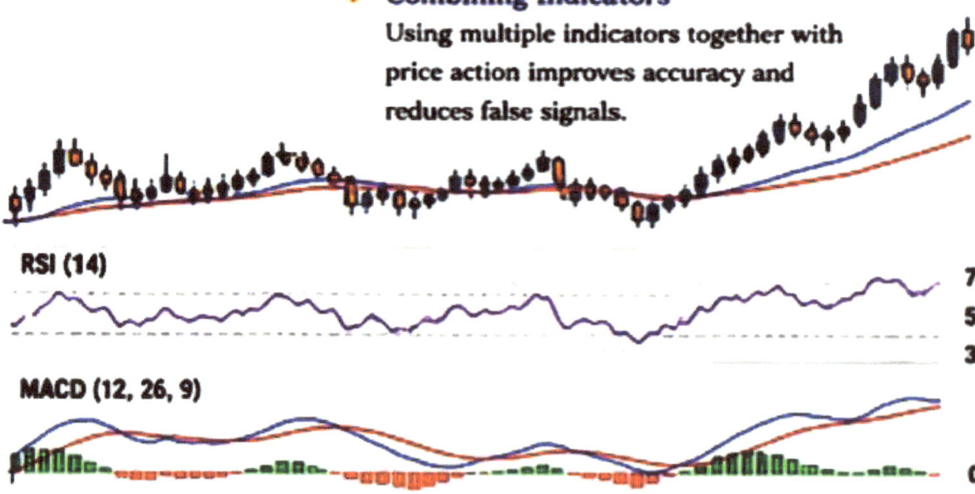

FINAL THOUGHT

Technical indicators are not magic.

They are tools that help you understand the market better.

The more you learn how to use them correctly, the more confident and consistent you will become.

Stay disciplined, manage your risk, and keep improving every day.

> *Indicators give you information, but discipline gives you results.*

CHAPTER 7

TRADING PSYCHOLOGY

Mastering Your Mind in the Markets

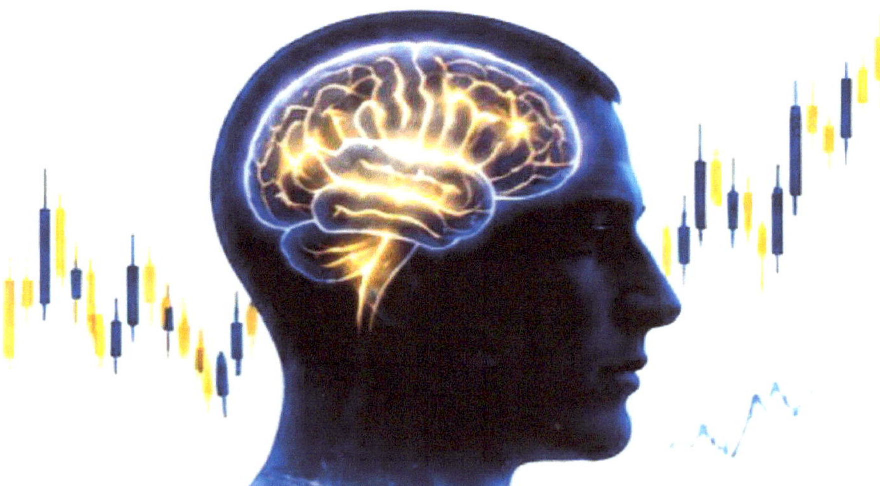

Successful trading is not just about strategies and indicators—it's about controlling your mindset. Your emotions, beliefs, and habits can either help you achieve consistency or sabotage your results. In this chapter, we explore the psychology behind trading and how to develop the mental discipline needed to thrive in the markets.

Why Psychology Matters

The financial markets test more than your knowledge—they test your emotions, patience, and discipline. Two traders with the same strategy can have completely different results because of their mindset.

Psychology affects every part of your trading:

- **Decision Making:** Emotions can cloud judgment and lead to poor choices.
- **Consistency:** A strong mindset helps you stick to your plan.
- **Risk Management:** Emotional control prevents overtrading and revenge trading.
- **Resilience:** The right mindset helps you learn from losses and keep going.

Mastering your psychology gives you an edge that no strategy alone can provide.

Fear and Greed

Fear and greed are the two most powerful emotions in trading. They can push you to make impulsive decisions that harm your account.

Fear can cause you to:

- Exit trades too early
- Avoid taking valid setups
- Hold losing trades hoping they will turn around

Greed can lead you to:

- Overtrade and take unnecessary risks
- Chase the market
- Ignore your trading plan

The key is not to eliminate these emotions, but to recognize them and manage them. Awareness brings control, and control leads to consistency.

Common Psychological Mistakes

Many traders struggle because of recurring mental mistakes. Here are some of the most common ones:

- **Revenge Trading:** Trying to win back losses quickly usually leads to bigger losses.
- **Overconfidence:** After a few wins, traders risk too much and ignore their plan.
- **FOMO (Fear of Missing Out):** Jumping into trades without a plan because of fear of missing an opportunity.
- **Impatience:** Forcing trades instead of waiting for high-probability setups.
- **Blaming Others:** Not taking responsibility prevents growth and improvement.

Recognizing these mistakes is the first step to breaking them. A strong trader works on their mindset every day.

Building Trading Discipline

Discipline is the foundation of long-term trading success. Without it, even the best strategy will fail.

Here's how to build strong discipline:

- **Follow Your Trading Plan:** Stick to your plan for every trade. It removes guesswork and emotions from the process.
- **Consistency Over Emotion:** Make decisions based on logic and strategy, not how you feel in the moment.
- **Develop Good Habits:** Create a routine that includes preparation, risk management, and review. Good habits lead to consistent results.

Discipline isn't about being perfect—it's about staying committed to your process, no matter what happens in the market.

MANAGING EMOTIONS

Emotions are a natural part of trading, but how you manage them makes all the difference.

Key steps to manage your emotions:

- **Stay Calm During Losses:** Losses are part of trading. Accept them, learn from them, and move on. Don't let them shake your confidence.
- **Avoid Impulsive Decisions:** Strong emotions can lead to rushed decisions. Pause, breathe, and stick to your plan.
- **Emotional Awareness:** Recognize how you feel before, during, and after trades. Awareness helps you take control instead of letting emotions take over.

When you manage your emotions, you make better decisions and protect your trading capital.

Developing a Trader's Mindset

A strong mindset sets successful traders apart from the rest. Focus on these key areas:

- **Patience:** Wait for the right setups. Good trades come to those who wait.
- **Confidence:** Believe in your strategy and your ability to execute it. Confidence comes from preparation and experience.
- **Continuous Learning:** The markets are always changing. Keep learning, adapting, and improving your skills.
- **Long-Term Thinking:** Focus on long-term growth, not quick wins. Consistency over time builds true success.

Developing the right mindset takes time, but it's the key to lasting success in trading.

Chapter Summary

In this chapter, we explored the critical role of psychology in trading:

- **Psychology Matters:** Your mindset affects every decision and outcome.
- **Fear and Greed:** These emotions can lead to poor decisions if left unchecked.
- **Discipline:** Sticking to your plan and building good habits leads to consistency.
- **Emotional Control:** Managing emotions helps you stay calm and make better choices.
- **Consistency:** A strong mindset and consistent actions create long-term success.

Master your mind, and you'll master your trading journey.

Final Thought

Trading is as much a mental game as it is a strategic one. Your mindset will always be tested, but with the right awareness, discipline, and emotional control, you can master yourself before you ever master the markets.

Remember, the goal isn't to be perfect—it's to be consistent. Focus on controlling what you can: your thoughts, your emotions, and your actions. When you do, the results will take care of themselves.

Keep growing, keep learning, and trust the process.

"The mind is everything. What you think you become."

— Buddha

Chapter 8

Risk Management

Protecting Your Capital

No matter how good your strategy is, one bad trade can cause serious damage if you don't manage your risk. Risk management is the key to long-term survival and consistent success in trading.

In this chapter, you'll learn how to protect your capital, control losses, and trade in a way that gives you the best chance to grow your account over time.

Why Risk Management Matters

Risk management is the foundation of every successful trader. Here's why it's so important:

- **Protects Your Capital:** Your capital is your tool for trading. Protecting it allows you to stay in the game and take advantage of future opportunities.

- **Ensures Long-Term Survival:** Trading is a marathon, not a sprint. Good risk management keeps you consistent and in the market longer.

- **Improves Risk vs. Reward:** By managing risk effectively, you can aim for high-quality trades with better potential rewards.

- **Prevents Big Losses:** Even a few big losses can wipe out your account. Managing risk helps you avoid disasters.

Successful traders focus on how much they can lose, not just how much they can make.

Position Sizing Basics

Position sizing is how you decide how much of your capital to risk on a single trade.

Key principles:

- **Risk a Small Percentage:** Most traders risk only 1–2% of their capital per trade. This keeps losses small and manageable.
- **Adjust Position Size:** The bigger the risk (stops are wider), the smaller your position size should be.
- **Be Consistent:** Using the same risk rules for every trade helps you stay disciplined.
- **Example:** If you have $10,000 and risk 1% per trade, that's $100. If your stop loss is $1 away, you can trade 100 shares.

Proper position sizing protects your account and allows you to stay consistent, even during losing streaks.

Risk-to-Reward Ratio

The risk-to-reward ratio helps you compare how much you can lose on a trade versus how much you can potentially gain.

Key points:

- **What It Means:** It's the relationship between your potential loss (risk) and potential profit (reward) on a trade.
- **Common Ratios:** Many successful traders use at least 1:2 or 1:3. This means risking $1 to make $2 or $3.
- **Why It Matters:** A good ratio allows you to be profitable even if you're wrong more often than you're right.
- **Example:** Risk $100 to make $300 (1:3). Even if you win only 40% of your trades, you can still make a profit.

Focus on high-quality setups with favorable risk-to-reward ratios. It's the key to consistent long-term success.

Stop Losses

A stop loss is an order you place to exit a trade automatically if the market moves against you.

Key points:

- **Purpose:** Stop losses protect your capital and prevent small losses from becoming big ones.
- **Types of Stop Losses:**
  - **Fixed Stop Loss:** Set at a specific price level based on your risk.
  - **Technical Stop Loss:** Set below support levels (for long trades) or above resistance levels (for short trades).
- **Why Use Them:** They remove emotion from your decision-making and keep you disciplined.
- **Remember:** Every trade should have a stop loss before you enter.

A stop loss doesn't guarantee you won't lose, but it ensures you control how much you lose.

Take Profit Levels

Take profit levels help you lock in gains and stay disciplined in your trading.

Key points:

- **Purpose:** They help you exit a trade when your target is reached, securing your profits.
- **Plan Ahead:** Always set your take profit level before entering the trade.
- **Use Risk-to-Reward:** Base your target on your risk-to-reward ratio. For example, if you risk $100, aim to make $200 or $300.
- **Avoid Greed:** Markets can reverse at any time. Taking profits removes greed and protects your gains.

A good trader knows when to take profits and move on to the next opportunity.

Managing Drawdowns

Drawdowns are a normal part of trading. Managing them well is what separates successful traders from the rest.

Key points:

- **What Is a Drawdown:** It's a reduction in your account balance from a peak to a low point.
- **Accept It:** No trader wins every trade. Losing streaks will happen.
- **Reduce Position Size:** During drawdowns, consider reducing your position size to limit further losses.
- **Stay Disciplined:** Stick to your plan and avoid trying to win back losses quickly.
- **Focus on Consistency:** Small, consistent gains over time are better than big, risky wins.

The goal is not to avoid drawdowns, but to manage them and recover stronger.

Common Risk Management Mistakes

Even experienced traders make mistakes. Here are some common risk management mistakes to avoid:

- **Risking Too Much:** Risking a large portion of your account on a single trade can lead to significant losses.
- **No Stop-Loss:** Entering trades without a stop-loss is like driving without brakes.
- **Overtrading:** Taking too many trades increases costs and reduces focus.
- **Ignoring the Plan:** Not following your trading plan leads to impulsive and emotional decisions.
- **Revenge Trading:** Trying to win back losses quickly often results in even bigger losses.

Avoiding these mistakes can protect your capital and improve your long-term performance.

Building a Risk Management Plan

A solid risk management plan is essential for consistent trading success. Here's how to build one:

- **Define Your Risk Per Trade:** Decide the maximum percentage of your account you are willing to risk on each trade.
- **Set Stop-Loss Levels:** Determine logical stop-loss levels based on support, resistance, or volatility.
- **Determine Position Size:** Calculate your position size based on your risk per trade and stop-loss distance.
- **Set Profit Targets:** Define realistic profit targets and use risk-reward ratios.
- **Review and Adjust:** Regularly review your plan and adjust based on performance and market conditions.

A well-planned trade is a controlled risk.

Chapter Summary

In this chapter, we explored the importance of risk management in trading:

- **Protecting Capital:** Risk management helps preserve your capital and keeps you in the game longer.
- **Limiting Losses:** Using stop-loss orders and proper position sizing limits potential losses.
- **Consistency:** Managing risk helps you stay consistent and avoid emotional decisions.
- **Long-Term Success:** Good risk management is the foundation of long-term trading success.

Remember, it's not about how much you make, but how much you keep.

FINAL THOUGHT

Risk management is not just a set of rules; it's a mindset. It's what separates consistent traders from those who struggle.

You can have the best strategy in the world, but without proper risk management, you won't last long in the markets.

Protect your capital, control your emotions, and stay disciplined. The market will always be there, but your capital might not.

Trade smart, manage risk, and let consistency lead you to success.

CHAPTER 9

TRADING STRATEGIES

Mastering Different Approaches to the Market

A trading strategy is a structured plan for entering trades, managing them, and exiting with a profit. The right strategy helps remove emotion from decision-making and provides a clear path toward consistent results.

In this chapter, you'll learn several popular trading strategies used by traders to identify opportunities, manage risk, and adapt to changing market conditions.

Trend Following Strategy

The trend following strategy is based on the idea that markets move in trends and tend to continue in that direction.

How It Works:

- Identify the trend using moving averages, trendlines, or price action.
- Buy in an uptrend and sell in a downtrend.
- Ride the trend until there are signs of reversal.

Best Used In:

Strong trending markets.

Key Tips:

- Use higher timeframes to identify the trend.
- Place stop-loss below support (in uptrend) or above resistance (in downtrend).
- Let profits run and avoid exiting too early.

Trend following works because the market rewards patience and discipline.

BREAKOUT STRATEGY

The breakout strategy is based on entering a trade when price breaks through a key support or resistance level with strong momentum.

How It Works:

- Identify key support and resistance zones.
- Wait for price to break out of the zone.
- Enter the trade in the direction of the breakout.
- Confirm the breakout with volume or price action.

Best Used In:

Range-bound markets and during news events.

Key Tips:

- False breakouts are common—wait for confirmation.
- Place stop-loss below support (long trades) or above resistance (short trades).
- Set realistic profit targets based on the range or volatility.

Breakouts can lead to strong moves when timed and executed correctly.

Reversal Strategy

The reversal strategy is used to identify potential trend reversals and enter trades at the beginning of a new trend.

How It Works:

- Identify overbought or oversold conditions using indicators like RSI, Stochastic, or price action.
- Look for reversal candlestick patterns.
- Enter the trade in the opposite direction of the current trend.

Best Used In:

Markets that are overextended or showing signs of a trend change.

Key Tips:

- Always wait for confirmation before entering.
- Use tight stop-loss to manage risk.
- Combine with support/resistance for higher accuracy.

Reversal trading requires patience and sharp analysis, but it can offer high-reward opportunities.

Scalping Basics

Scalping is a short-term trading strategy where traders aim to make small profits from minor price movements.

What Scalping Is:

Scalping involves taking multiple trades during the day and holding each trade for a few minutes to a few candles only.

Key Points:

- Focus on fast entries and exits.
- Capture small profits from small price movements.
- Profits are small per trade, but repeated frequently.
- Requires full attention and quick decision-making.

Risk Management for Scalpers:

- Use tight stop-loss to limit risk.
- Risk only a small percentage of your capital on each trade.
- Avoid overtrading; quality setups are more important than quantity.
- Stay disciplined and follow your plan.

Scalping rewards speed, discipline, and consistency.

SWING TRADING

Swing trading is a style of trading that aims to capture short to medium-term moves in a stock over several days.

Key Features:

- Trades are held for several days to a few weeks.
- Focus on capturing larger price movements.
- Less screen time compared to intraday trading.
- Uses technical analysis to find high-probability setups.

How It Works:

- Identify a stock in an uptrend or downtrend.
- Use support and resistance levels to plan entries and exits.
- Enter near support in an uptrend or near resistance in a downtrend.
- Hold the trade until the trend shows signs of reversal.

Risk and Reward Considerations:

- Use wider stop-loss to allow for normal market fluctuations.
- Aim for a reward that is at least 2 to 3 times your risk.
- Manage position size based on your risk tolerance.

Swing trading suits traders who prefer a balanced approach between time and results.

VWAP + EMA 7

Breakout Strategy

Time Frame: 15 Minutes

Indicators Used:

- VWAP (Volume Weighted Average Price)
- EMA 7 (7-Period Exponential Moving Average)

This strategy helps identify strong bullish momentum during the market open.

Setup:

1. Observe the first 15-minute candle after the market opens (9:15–9:30 AM).
2. The candle should close bullish (green).
3. VWAP should be moving through the candle and trending upward.
4. EMA 7 should remain below the price, indicating bullish strength.

Entry Rules:

1. Draw a horizontal line at the high of the first bullish 15-minute candle.
2. Wait for a later candle to break above this resistance level.
3. Do not enter immediately after the breakout.
4. Wait for the next candle to close above the resistance level as confirmation.
5. Enter a buy trade above the high of the confirmation candle.

Stop-Loss:

Place the stop-loss below the low of the confirmation candle.

Trade Logic:

This strategy aims to capture stocks showing early strength, supported by VWAP and EMA alignment. Waiting for confirmation helps reduce false breakouts and improves trade quality.

GAP-UP OPENING BREAKOUT STRATEGY

Time Frame: 15 Minutes

Strategy Overview

This strategy focuses on stocks that open with a significant gap-up and show strong buying interest during the first trading session of the day.

Setup:

1. Identify a stock that opens with a gap-up compared to the previous trading day's closing price.
2. The first 15-minute candle should close bullish (green).
3. Trading volume during the first candle should be higher than the stock's average volume.
4. These conditions indicate strong market participation and potential bullish momentum.

Entry Rules:

1. Draw a horizontal resistance line at the high of the first 15-minute candle.
2. Wait for a subsequent candle to break above this resistance level.
3. Do not enter immediately on the breakout.
4. Wait for confirmation from the next candle closing above the resistance.
5. Enter a buy trade above the high of the confirmation candle.

Stop-Loss:

Place the stop-loss below the low of the confirmation candle.

Trade Logic:

A gap-up combined with strong volume often signals institutional buying interest. Waiting for a confirmed breakout helps avoid false signals and increases the probability of entering a strong trend.

FIBONACCI RETRACEMENT STRATEGY

Strategy Overview

Fibonacci Retracement is a popular tool used to identify potential support and resistance levels during a trend. It helps traders find high-probability entry points by locating areas where price is likely to pull back before continuing in the direction of the trend.

When the Market Is Moving Up

1. Draw Fibonacci retracement from the recent swing low to the recent swing high.
2. Key retracement levels to watch: 23.6%, 38.2%, 50%, 61.8%, and 78.6%.
3. Look for buying opportunities near the 38.2% or 61.8% level.
4. Wait for a bullish price action or candlestick pattern for confirmation.

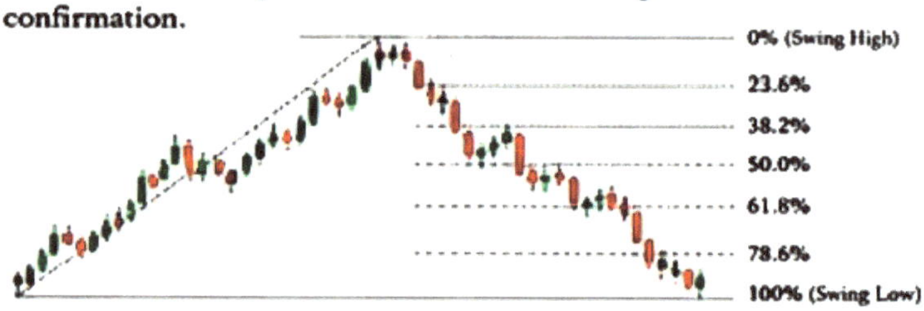

When the Market Is Moving Down

1. Draw Fibonacci retracement from the recent swing high to the recent swing low.
2. Key retracement levels to watch: 23.6%, 38.2%, 50%, 61.8%, and 78.6%.
3. Look for selling opportunities near the 38.2% or 61.8% level.
4. Wait for a bearish price action or candlestick pattern for confirmation.

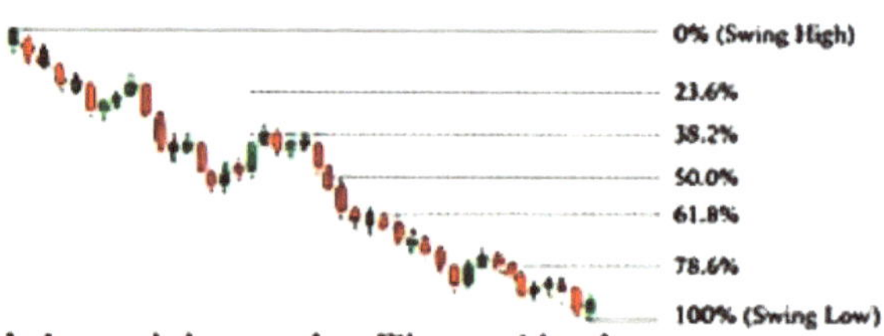

Stop-Loss

Place the stop-loss slightly beyond the next key Fibonacci level.

Trade Logic

Fibonacci levels act as potential support and resistance zones. Price often reacts at these levels before continuing in the trend direction. Using Fibonacci helps traders enter trades with better precision and risk control.

Morning Star & Evening Star Strategy

Morning Star Pattern

Pattern Formation

1. A long bearish (red) candle.
2. A small-bodied candle (can be red or green) that gaps down.
3. A long bullish (green) candle that closes well into the body of the first candle.

Entry Rule

Enter a buy trade above the high of the third (bullish) candle.

Evening Star Pattern

Pattern Formation

1. A long bullish (green) candle.
2. A small-bodied candle (can be red or green) that gaps up.
3. A long bearish (red) candle that closes well into the body of the first candle.

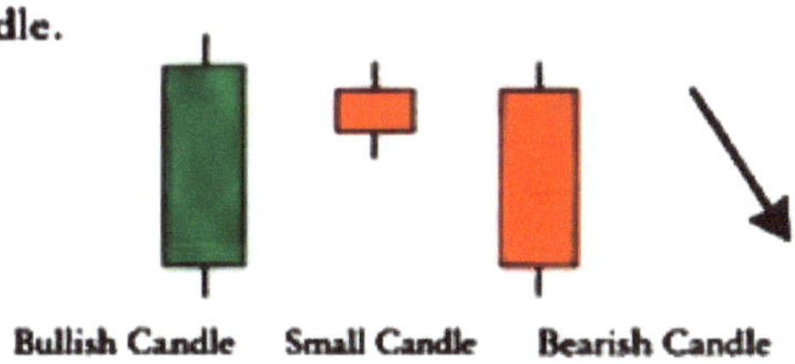

Entry Rule

Enter a sell trade below the low of the third (bearish) candle.

Trade Logic

These patterns indicate a potential reversal in trend. The first candle shows strong trend continuation, the second shows hesitation, and the third confirms the reversal as the opposite side takes control.

Donchian Channel Strategy

Trading Style: Intraday and Swing Trading

Time Frames: 5 Minutes and 15 Minutes

Donchian Channel Length: 22

Remove Basis (Middle Line)

Setup

1. Add Donchian Channel to the chart with a length of 22.
2. Remove the basis (middle line), so only the upper and lower bands are visible.
3. The upper band acts as resistance and the lower band acts as support.

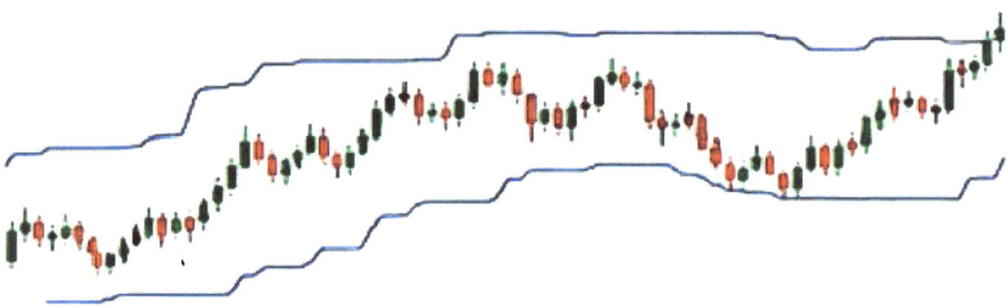

Entry Rule

Enter a buy trade when the price closes above the upper Donchian band with strong momentum.

Stop-Loss

Place the stop-loss at the lower Donchian band.

Trade Logic

Donchian Channel helps identify breakouts and trends. When price breaks above the upper band, it indicates strong buying momentum and the start of a potential uptrend. Using the lower band as a stop-loss keeps the risk well-defined.

Double Bottom Trading Strategy

Strategy Overview

The Double Bottom pattern is a bullish reversal pattern that forms after a downtrend. It indicates that sellers are losing strength and buyers are stepping in near a strong support zone, creating a potential upward reversal.

Setup

1. Identify a clear downtrend.
2. Look for a support zone where price touches and forms two distinct bottoms at roughly the same level.
3. A neckline (resistance line) forms between the two bottoms.
4. Wait for price to break above the neckline with strength.

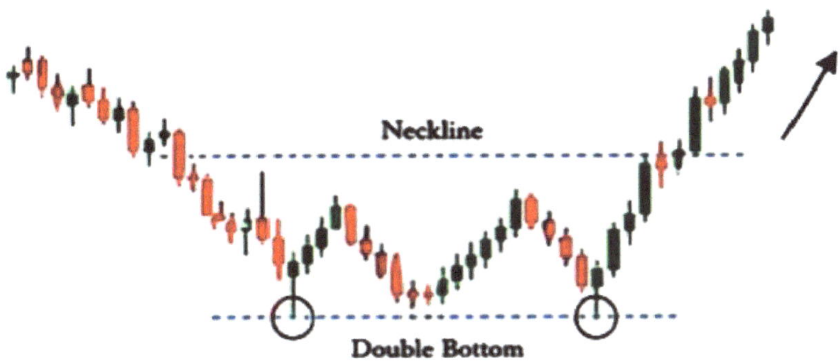

Entry Rule

Enter a buy trade above the neckline (resistance) high.

Stop-Loss

Place the stop-loss below the low of the second bottom.

Trade Logic

The Double Bottom shows strong support holding at a key level. A breakout above the neckline confirms buyer strength and can lead to a sustained uptrend.

Additional Observation (Nifty Midcap 100 Stocks)

Double Bottom patterns in Nifty Midcap 100 stocks often lead to strong momentum moves due to higher volatility and liquidity expansion. Breakouts backed by good volume tend to perform better and offer favorable risk-to-reward.

MA 47 Support Bounce Strategy

Time Frame: 30 Minutes

Indicator Used: Moving Average (MA 47)

Strategy Overview

This strategy looks for buying opportunities when price is in a downtrend and approaches a strong support zone far below the MA 47. A bullish reaction from that support zone with a bounce toward the MA 47 can offer a high-probability trade setup.

Setup

1. Apply the MA 47 indicator to the chart.
2. The MA 47 should be in a clear downtrend.
3. Price should be trading well below the MA 47.
4. Identify a strong support zone where price has reacted multiple times.

Entry Rules

1. Wait for price to touch the support zone.
2. Look for a bullish candle to form at the support zone.
3. Enter the trade above the high of the bullish confirmation candle.

Stop-Loss

Place the stop-loss below the low of the bullish confirmation candle.

Target

The target for this trade is the MA 47 line.

Trade Logic

When price is far below a downward sloping MA 47, it often bounces from a strong support zone and moves back toward the MA 47. This setup provides a good risk-to-reward opportunity.

Stochastic Crossover Strategy

Trading Style: Swing Trading

Time Frame: 30 Minutes

Indicator Used: Stochastic Oscillator (%K and %D)

Strategy Overview

The Stochastic Oscillator helps identify momentum shifts and potential reversals. This strategy focuses on bullish setups when %K crosses above %D near the oversold zone.

Setup

1. Apply the Stochastic Oscillator to the chart.
2. Monitor %K (blue line) and %D (red line).
3. Look for %K crossing above %D.
4. The crossover should occur near the lower limit (oversold area).

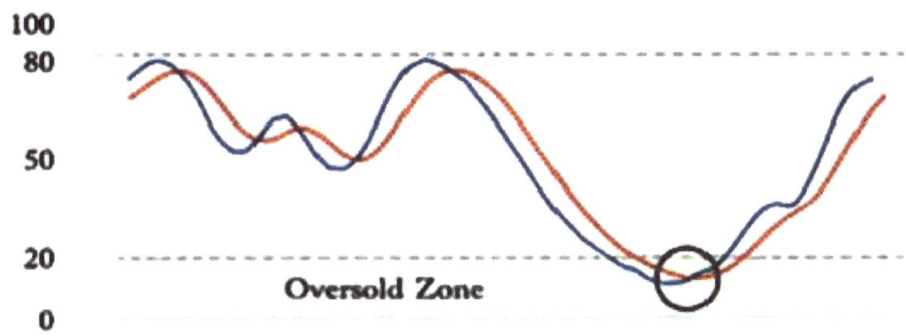

Entry Rules

1. Wait for %K to cross above %D.
2. Allow the lines to cross the lower limit (oversold zone).
3. After crossing the lower limit, wait for a bullish candle to form on the price chart.
4. Enter the trade above the high of the bullish confirmation candle.

Stop-Loss

Place the stop-loss below the nearest swing low.

Trade Logic

A bullish crossover near the oversold zone indicates that selling pressure may be weakening and buyers are gaining momentum. Using the nearest swing low as stop-loss allows better risk control while keeping enough room for the trade to develop.

MA 50 + Bollinger Band Bounce Strategy

Trading Style: Swing Trading

Time Frame: 5 Minutes

Indicators Used: Moving Average (MA 50) and Bollinger Bands (20)

Bollinger Band Settings

1. Open Bollinger Bands (20) settings.
2. Remove Upper Band.
3. Remove Basis (Middle Line).
4. Remove Background Fill.
5. Keep only Lower Band visible.

Strategy Overview

This strategy looks for bullish opportunities when the price is near a confluence of the MA 50 and the Lower Bollinger Band. Strong volume and a bullish candle at this zone can lead to a potential bounce and upward move.

Setup

1. Apply MA 50 and Bollinger Bands (20).
2. Ensure only the Lower Bollinger Band is visible.
3. Look for the MA 50 and Lower Bollinger Band to be very close to each other.
4. Volume of the stock should be higher than the average volume.

Entry Rules

1. Wait for a bullish candle to form near the MA 50 and Lower Bollinger Band area.
2. Confirm that the volume is more than the average volume.
3. Enter the trade above the high of the bullish candle.

Stop-Loss

Place the stop-loss below the low of the bullish confirmation candle.

Trade Logic

When MA 50 and the Lower Bollinger Band align closely, they act as a strong support zone. A bullish candle with high volume shows buying interest and can lead to a short-term upward move.

Williams %R + RSI + Stochastic + 10 EMA + 20 EMA Strategy

Type: Intraday

Time Frame: 5 Minutes

Indicators Used:

- Williams %R
- RSI
- Stochastic
- 10 EMA
- 20 EMA

Strategy Overview

This strategy combines three momentum oscillators and two moving averages to identify high-probability bullish reversal setups in the oversold zone. When all conditions align and price takes support on both EMAs, it signals a strong intraday buy opportunity.

Setup

1. Williams %R, RSI, and Stochastic are all in the oversold zone.
2. Price is in a short-term down move.
3. A bullish candle takes support on both the 10 EMA and 20 EMA.

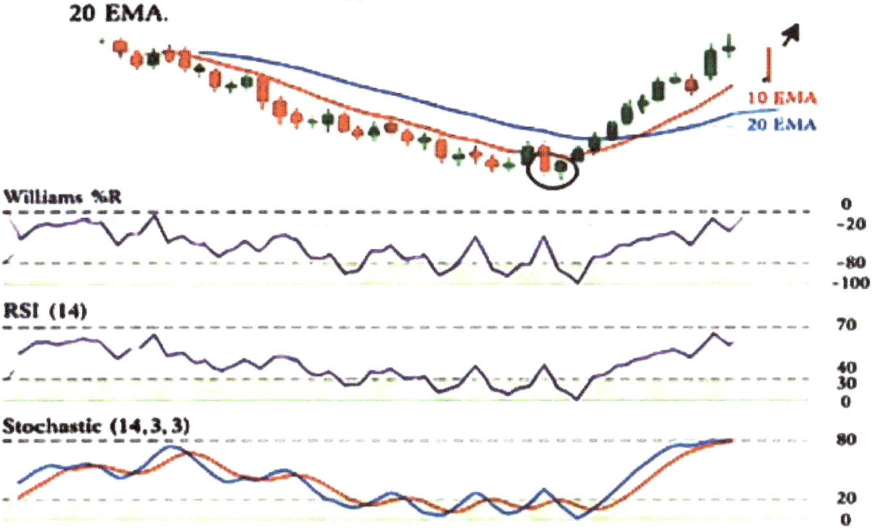

Entry Rules

1. Williams %R, RSI, and Stochastic must all be in the oversold zone.
2. Not one or two indicators; all three must be oversold.
3. A bullish candle must take support on both the 10 EMA and 20 EMA.

Stop-Loss

Place the stop-loss below the low of the confirmation candle.

Trade Logic

When all three indicators are oversold, it shows extreme selling pressure. If price holds and a bullish candle takes support on both EMAs, it indicates a potential trend reversal with bullish momentum building for an upward move.

RSI Divergence Strategy

Type: Intraday and Swing Trading

Time Frames:

- 5 Minutes (Intraday)
- 1 Day (Swing)

Strategy Overview

RSI Divergence is a powerful reversal strategy that identifies weakening selling pressure while price forms a higher low. When price makes a higher bottom but RSI makes a lower bottom, it shows bullish divergence, indicating a potential reversal to the upside.

Setup

1. Price forms a higher bottom.
2. RSI forms a lower bottom.
3. This creates bullish RSI divergence.

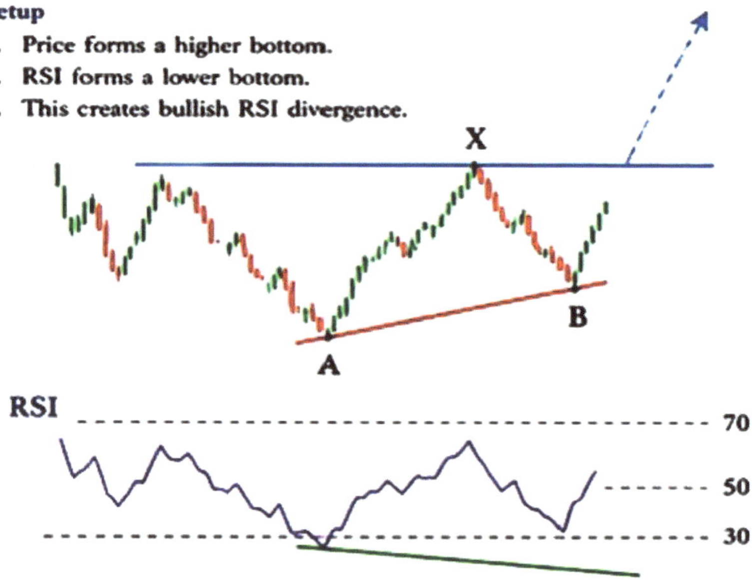

Entry Rules

1. Enter above the high of point X (resistance breakout).
2. Confirmation candle should close above point X.

Stop-Loss

Place the stop-loss below point B (the higher bottom low).

Target Formula

$$\text{Target} = X + (B - A)$$

Trade Logic

Divergence shows that the momentum of the downtrend is weakening while buyers are quietly accumulating. A breakout above X confirms a reversal and provides a high-probability move. The target formula projects the likely upside move based on the depth of the pattern.

VWAP + Bollinger Bands Strategy

Time Frame: 15 Minutes

Indicators Used:

- VWAP
- Bollinger Bands

Bollinger Band Settings

- Standard Deviation = 1
- Hide Basis (Middle Line)
- Hide Lower Band
- Keep Upper Band visible

Strategy Overview

This strategy uses VWAP and the Upper Bollinger Band to identify intraday momentum breakouts. When VWAP crosses above the Upper Bollinger Band and price retests VWAP with confirmation, it signals a strong bullish opportunity.

Setup

1. VWAP crosses above the Upper Bollinger Band from below.
2. This shows the start of bullish momentum.

Entry Rules

1. The second candle must take support on VWAP.
2. Check that VWAP remained flat for some time before the previous trading session closed.
3. The second candle must be bullish.
4. Enter above the high of the second candle.

Stop-Loss

Place the stop-loss below the low of the second candle.

Trade Logic

A flat VWAP before the session close shows balance and accumulation. When price breaks out, VWAP crossing above the Upper Band confirms strength. A retest of VWAP with a bullish candle shows buyers stepping in, increasing the probability of a strong upward move.

RSI + MACD Mixed Strategy

Type: Swing Trading

Time Frame: 1 Day

Indicators Used:

- RSI
- MACD

Strategy Overview

This strategy combines the strength of RSI and MACD to capture early uptrends. It ensures momentum shift (MACD) and strength confirmation (RSI) before taking a long position.

Setup

1. Stock starts showing upward movement.
2. MACD histogram turns green from red.
3. MACD lines remain below the zero line.
4. RSI line crosses above 40 from below.

MACD (12, 26, 9)

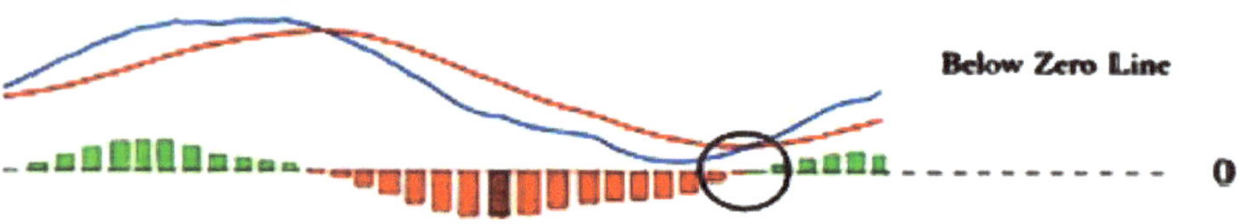

RSI (14)

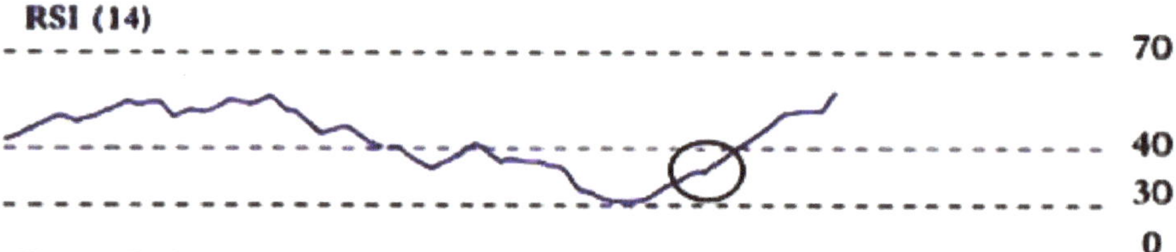

Entry Rules

1. Enter above the high of the signal candle.

Stop-Loss

Place the stop-loss below the low of the previous candle.

Trade Logic

MACD turning green from red shows momentum shift while still below zero (early trend). RSI crossing above 40 confirms strength and buyer control. This combination improves the probability of a sustained upward move.

Positive Reverse Divergence (PRD) & Negative Reverse Divergence (NRD) Strategy

Type: Intraday and Swing Trading

Positive Reverse Divergence (PRD)

Setup

1. Price forms a Lower Low.
2. Indicator forms a Higher High.
3. Volume should be higher than average.
4. This indicates underlying strength and a possible bullish reversal.

Entry Rule

Enter above the high of the bullish confirmation candle.

Stop-Loss

Below the recent swing low.

Trade Logic

When price makes a lower low but the indicator makes a higher high, it shows hidden strength in the market. Higher than average volume increases the probability of a bullish reversal or continuation.

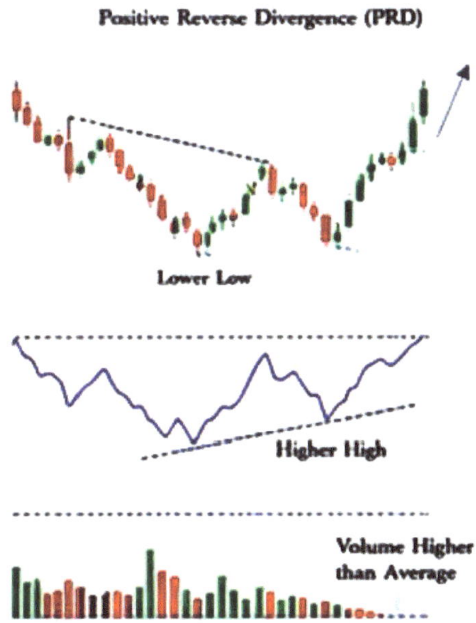

Negative Reverse Divergence (NRD)

Setup

1. Price forms a Higher High.
2. Indicator forms a Lower High.
3. This indicates weakening momentum and a possible bearish reversal.

Entry Rule

Enter below the low of the bearish confirmation candle.

Stop-Loss

Above the recent swing high.

Trade Logic

When price makes a higher high but the indicator makes a lower high, it shows hidden weakness in the market. This increases the probability of a bearish reversal or continuation.

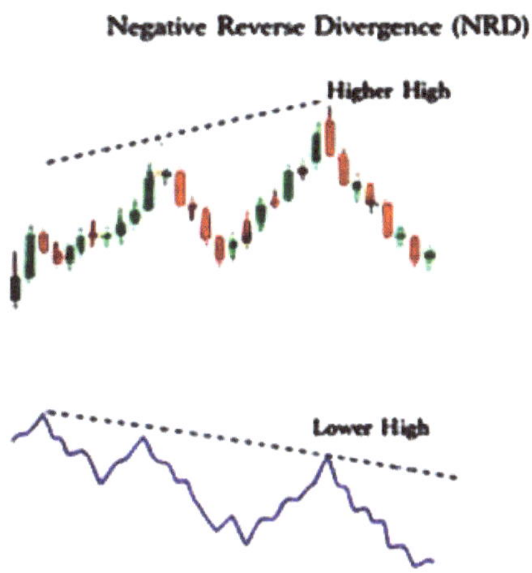

GAP-UP FIRST 30 MINUTES BREAKOUT STRATEGY

Type: Intraday Trading

Time Frame: 15 Minutes

Strategy Overview

This strategy uses the first 30 minutes of the market after a gap-up opening to identify key levels and trade the breakout in the direction of the trend.

Setup

1. Look for a stock that opens with a gap-up.
2. Observe the first two 15-minute candles.
3. Mark the following levels:
   - Resistance = High of Second Candle
   - Support = Low of First Candle
4. These levels help identify the trend in the first 30 minutes.

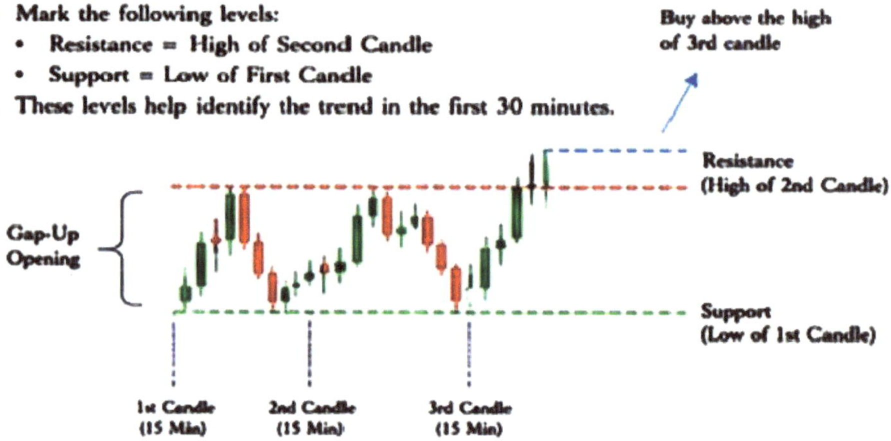

Entry Rule

- Buy above the high of the third candle after the price breaks above the resistance level.

Stop-Loss Options

- Option 1 (Aggressive): Below the low of the third candle.
- Option 2 (Conservative): Below the low of the first candle.

Risk-to-Reward Ratio

Follow 1:3 Risk-to-Reward Ratio.

Target

Target = Entry Price + (3 × Risk)

Trade Logic

A gap-up opening shows strong buying interest. The first 30 minutes help create important support and resistance zones. A breakout above resistance often leads to continuation of the bullish momentum. Using a defined stop-loss and 1:3 risk-reward keeps the trade structured and disciplined.

SMMA Options Put Strategy

Type: Intraday Options Trading (Put)

Time Frame: 3 Minutes

Indicators Used:

- SMMA 11
- SMMA 21

Setup

1. Add SMMA 11 and SMMA 21 on the chart.
2. Wait until 10:00 A.M.
3. At or around 10:00 A.M., SMMA 11 crosses below SMMA 21 from up to down.
4. A red (bearish) candle forms at the time of the crossover.
5. A swing low is formed.
6. Wait for one more swing low to form.
7. Then wait for price to pull back and touch the SMMA 11.
8. A red candle forms as it touches the SMMA 11.

Entry Rules

Enter a Put option trade at the low of that red candle.

Stop-Loss

Place stop-loss at the SMMA 21.

> **Important Note**
>
> - Use this strategy only between 10:00 A.M. and 12:00 Noon.
> - Do not use this strategy after 12:00 Noon.

Trade Logic

When SMMA 11 crosses below SMMA 21 with a bearish candle, it shows a shift in momentum to the downside. Consecutive swing lows confirm selling pressure. A pullback to SMMA 11 followed by a bearish candle gives a low-risk entry in the direction of the trend.

Camarilla Pivot Trading Strategy

Type: Intraday Trading

Time Frame: 5 Minutes

Indicator:

- Pivot Points Standard

Settings

1. Add Pivot Points Standard to the chart.
2. From its input settings, select Camarilla.
3. From Styles, remove the following levels:
   - P (Pivot)
   - S1 / R1
   - S2 / R2
4. Keep only the following levels visible:
   - S3
   - R3
   - S4
   - R4

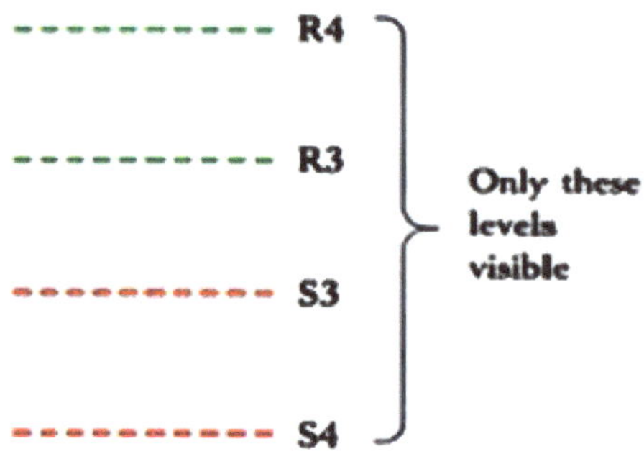

Setup

1. Wait for price to reach the S3 level.
2. Observe the price action carefully at S3.
3. A red candle should form with its wick crossing below the S3 line.

Confirmation

1. After the red candle, a green candle must form.
2. The green candle's high should be equal to or above the high of the red candle.
3. This shows buyers are defending the S3 support area.

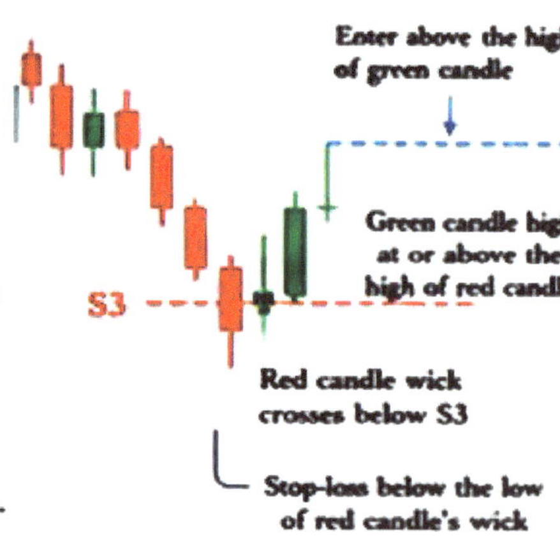

Entry Rule

Enter above the high of the green confirmation candle.

Stop-Loss

Place stop-loss below the low of the red candle's wick.

Trade Logic

The Camarilla S3 level acts as a strong intraday support. When price rejects below S3 and buyers step in (green candle with higher high), it increases the probability of a bounce towards higher levels like R3.

TREND FOLLOWING MA STRATEGY

Time Frame: 1 Hour

Indicator Used: Moving Average (MA 20)

Strategy Overview

This strategy aims to capture strong trends by following the price in the direction of the MA 20. It works well in trending markets and helps traders ride the momentum.

Setup

1. Add the MA 20 to the chart.
2. Price should be above the MA 20 for a bullish setup.
3. Price should be below the MA 20 for a bearish setup.
4. Look for a strong momentum candle in the trend direction.

Entry Rules

1. Wait for price to be above the MA 20.
2. Look for a bullish candle to form above the MA 20.
3. Enter the trade above the high of the bullish candle.

Stop-Loss

Place the stop-loss below the MA 20 or the recent swing low.

Target

Use a risk-to-reward ratio of at least 1:2 or trail the MA 20.

Trade Logic

In a strong uptrend, price tends to stay above the MA 20 and bounces off it. Following the trend increases the probability of success and helps capture extended moves.

Breakout Trading Strategy

Time Frame: 15 Minutes to 1 Hour

Indicator Used: Support & Resistance Levels

Strategy Overview

This strategy focuses on trading breakouts from key support and resistance levels. When price breaks a strong level with volume, it often continues in that direction.

Setup

1. Identify a strong support or resistance level.
2. Wait for price to approach the level.
3. Look for a breakout with high volume.
4. Confirm the breakout with a strong candle close.

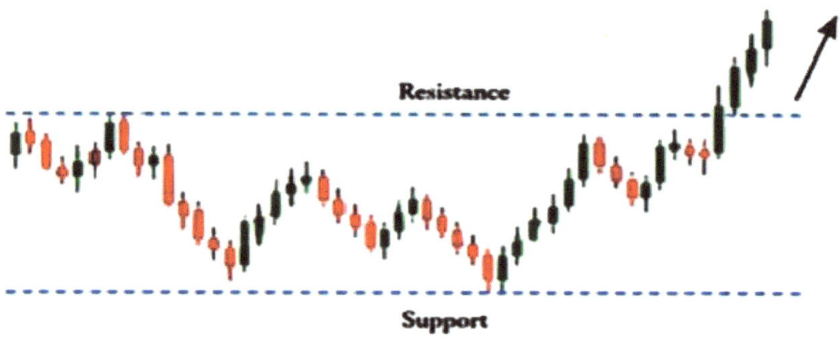

Entry Rules

1. Buy above resistance after a strong breakout.
2. Sell below support after a strong breakdown.
3. Enter the trade above the high (buy) or below the low (sell) of the breakout candle.

Stop-Loss

Place the stop-loss below support (buy) or above resistance (sell).

Target

Use a risk-to-reward ratio of at least 1:2 or next key level.

Trade Logic

Breakouts indicate that the price has gained strength and is likely to continue moving in the breakout direction, offering high-probability opportunities.

RSI Overbought Oversold Strategy

Time Frame: 15 Minutes

Indicator Used: Relative Strength Index (RSI 14)

Strategy Overview

This strategy uses the RSI indicator to identify overbought and oversold conditions. It helps traders find potential reversal points in the market.

Setup

1. Add RSI (14) to the chart.
2. RSI above 70 indicates overbought.
3. RSI below 30 indicates oversold.
4. Look for a reversal candle at these zones.

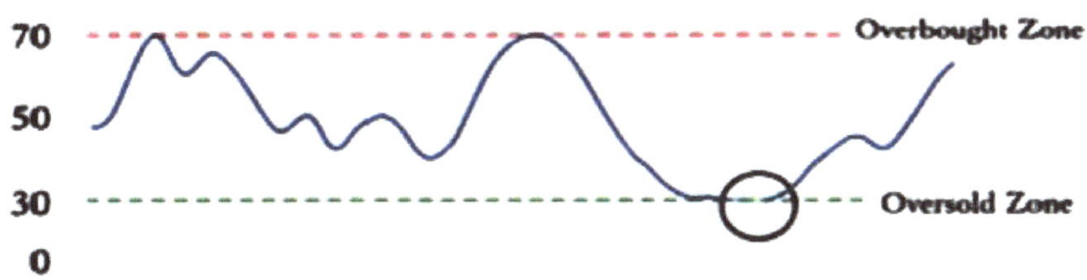

Entry Rules

1. When RSI is below 30, wait for a bullish reversal candle.
2. When RSI is above 70, wait for a bearish reversal candle.
3. Enter the trade above the high (buy) or below the low (sell) of the reversal candle.

Stop-Loss

Place the stop-loss below the recent swing low (buy) or above the recent swing high (sell).

Target

Use a risk-to-reward ratio of at least 1:2.

Trade Logic

RSI extremes show that the market may be overextended and a reversal is likely. Combining RSI with price action increases the accuracy of the setups.

INSIDE BAR BREAKOUT STRATEGY

Time Frame: 1 Hour to 4 Hour

Indicator Used: Price Action

Strategy Overview

Inside Bar Breakout strategy identifies periods of consolidation and trades the breakout in the direction of the next strong move.

Setup

1. Identify an inside bar (small candle inside the previous candle).
2. Wait for the price to break the high or low of the inside bar.
3. Look for a strong candle closing outside the range.
4. Confirm with volume or momentum.

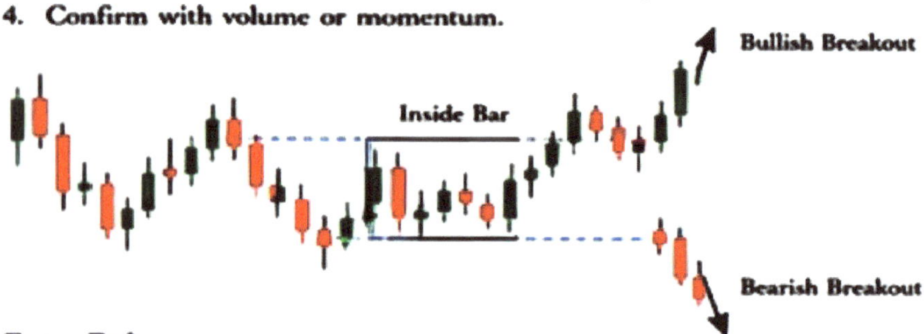

Entry Rules

1. Buy above the high of the inside bar.
2. Sell below the low of the inside bar.
3. Enter the trade when the breakout candle closes.

Stop-Loss

Place the stop-loss below the inside bar low (buy) or above the inside bar high (sell).

Target

Use a risk-to-reward ratio of at least 1:2 or next key level.

Trade Logic

Inside bars show market consolidation. A breakout confirms the continuation of the trend and offers a high-probability trading opportunity.

ELLIOTT WAVE THEORY STRATEGY

Type: Any

Time Frame: According to the type

Strategy Overview:

It runs in 5 impulse waves.

- In which 1, 3 and 5 takes price up and 2 and 4 takes price down.
- After the wave 5 stock starts going down.

Setup:

1. Whenever you found a very small rally after a downtrend that is forming 1st wave and then takes pull back that is forming 2nd wave and then again starts going up.
2. Wait until it breaks the wave 1 high.

Entry Rule:

As it breaks the high of wave 1 take entry above the high of the candle high is broken.

Stop-Loss:

Low should be stoploss.

Target:

Then you have to hold until it reaches wave 5.

Trade Logic:

Elliott Wave Theory suggests that markets move in a natural pattern of 5 impulse waves. Entering after the wave 1 high breakout helps in capturing the powerful wave 3, which usually travels the longest.

Note:

If you are doing an intraday trade don't wait for the stock to make full wave 5 come out of the stock by 3:30 otherwise you will be squared off.

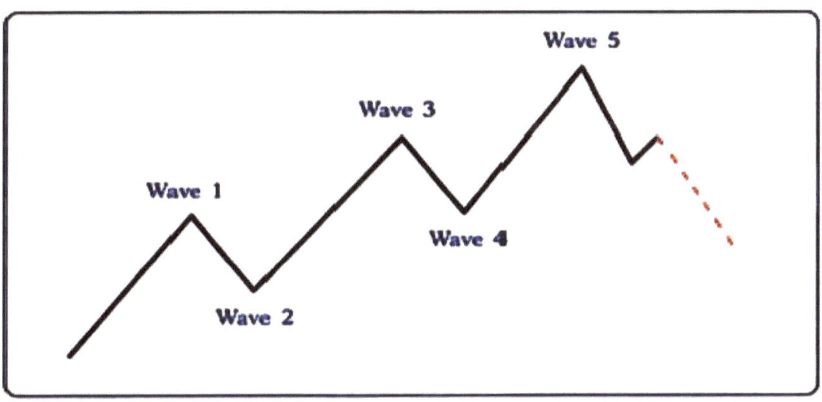

RSI + EMA 30
Reversal Strategy

Type: Any

Time Frame: According to the type

Strategy Overview:

This strategy helps to find potential reversal in a downtrend using EMA 30 and RSI near 60 level.

Setup:

1. Stock should already be In a downtrend.
2. It shows a small rally and creates a swing high by crossing the ema30 from down to up and after that again makes a swing low which is on 30 ema.
3. If you found these things matching look at RSI is it 60 or near 60 if yes again look at the candles are they making a bullish candle.

Entry Rule:

If yes buy above the high of the bullish candle.

Stop-Loss:

Low should be stoploss.

Target:

You will put is the swing high made before.

Trade Logic:

In a downtrend, price often retests the EMA 30 from below. When RSI is near 60 and a bullish candle forms, it indicates strength and possible reversal towards the previous swing high.

Note:

Don't wait for the target to hit if you are doing an intraday trade if your target is not hit till now then come out before 3:30 otherwise you will be squared off.

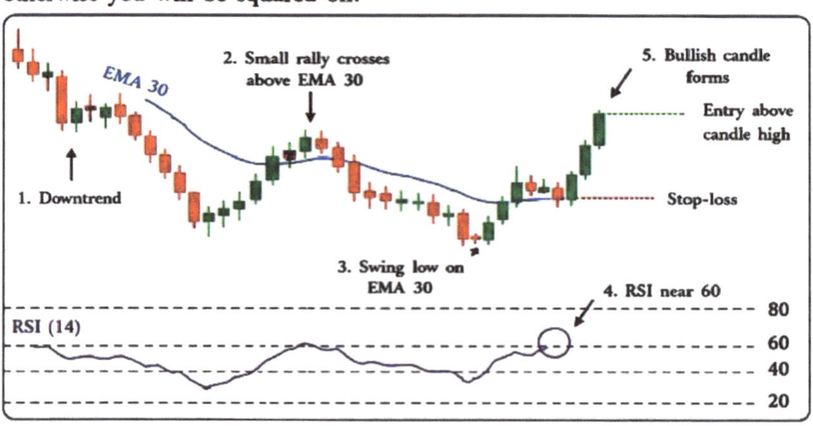

Power of One Red Candle Strategy

Time Frame: Any (according to trading style)

Type: Any (according to trading style)

Indicators Used: RSI

RSI Settings:

- Upper band 60
- Middle band 40
- Lower band 20

Strategy Overview:

Whenever any stock is showing rally from before and then forms a red candle that red can be the buying candle.
There are the steps for understanding of that candle.

Setup:

1. Stock should be In an uptrend.
2. RSI should be above 60.
3. Stock starts coming down.
4. RSI takes support on 60.
5. Buy on that red candle on which RSI is taking support on 60.

But:

There is one more acception if it is confirmed then only you will buy.

- It should be price's first small downtrend and RSI taking support on 60 after the big uptrend which means it should be price's first time taking support.

Entry Rule:

Buy on that red candle on which RSI is taking support on 60.

Stop-Loss:

Below the low of that red candle.

Target:

Previous swing high or as per your risk-reward.

Trade Logic:

When price pulls back for the first time in an uptrend and RSI takes support on 60, it shows buyers are still strong. The red candle is the best buying opportunity in that setup.

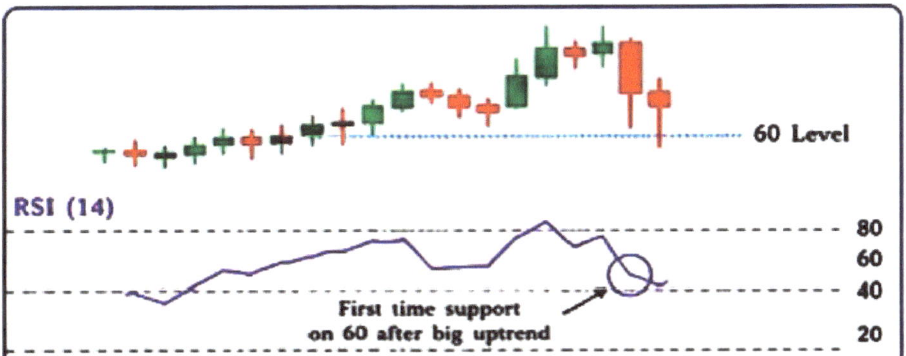

Back-to-Back 3 Red Candles
Long-Term Investing Strategy

Time Frame: 1 Month

Type: Long-Term Investing

Strategy Overview:

Whenever you found back to back 3 red candles with very small wick or no wick and after those red candles a green candle forms take entry above the high of that candle and low should be stop loss.

Setup:

1. Look for 3 consecutive red monthly candles.
2. The red candles should have very small wicks or no wicks.
3. After the third red candle, a green candle forms.

Entry Rule:

Take entry above the high of the green candle.

Stop-Loss:

Low should be stop loss.

Target:

As per your risk-reward or previous swing high.

Trade Logic:

Three strong red candles show heavy selling and weakness. When a green candle appears after them, it indicates buyers are back. Entering above the green candle high gives a strong long-term investment opportunity.

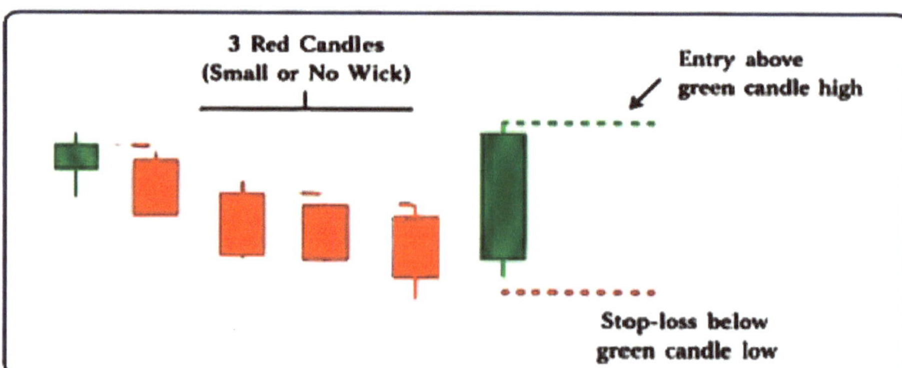

RSI + SUPERTREND + EMA STRATEGY

Time Frame: 1 Day

Type: Swing

Indicators Settings:

RSI:

- Upper limit - 60
- Middle limit - 40
- Lower limit - 20

Ema: Length - 15

Supertrend: No change

Strategy Overview:

Whenever you found that supertrend is in green and RSI is near or at 60 not below 40 understood that you have double confirmation now you only want the signal you will get it through ema as any green candle takes support on 15 ema atek entry above the high and low stop loss of that candle.

Setup:

1. Supertrend should be in green.
2. RSI should be near or at 60 and must not be below 40.
3. These two conditions give double confirmation.
4. Wait for price to come near or take support on 15 EMA.

Entry Rule:

- Wait for a green bullish candle to take support on the 15 EMA.
- Enter above the high of that green candle.

Stop-Loss:

- Place stop-loss below the low of that candle.

Target:

- Trail the position with Supertrend or exit at key resistance levels.

Trade Logic:

Supertrend in green confirms the trend, RSI near or at 60 confirms strength, and price taking support on 15 EMA gives the entry signal.
This combination increases the probability of a successful swing trade.

EMA CROSS STRATEGY

Time Frame: 5 Minutes
Type: Intraday
Indicators Used: EMA

Indicator Settings

Input

- EMA 1: Length 10
- EMA 2: Length 20

Style

- Remove every other indicator and keep only EMA 10 and EMA 20.
- (Alternatively, add EMA twice and set one length to 10 and the other to 20.)

Strategy Overview

This strategy is mainly useful when today's market opens below the previous day's closing price. It identifies bullish momentum using an EMA crossover.

Setup

1. Today's opening price should be lower than the previous session's closing price.
2. Apply EMA 10 and EMA 20.
3. Wait for EMA 10 to cross above EMA 20.
4. Wait for a green candle to take support on the EMA crossover.

Entry Rule

Buy above the high of the green candle taking support on EMA 10 and EMA 20.

Stop-Loss

Place the stop-loss below the low of the entry candle.

Target

Use your preferred risk-to-reward ratio or the next important resistance level.

Trade Logic

The EMA 10 crossing above EMA 20 indicates bullish momentum.
A green candle taking support on the EMA confirms buying strength and provides a high-probability intraday entry.

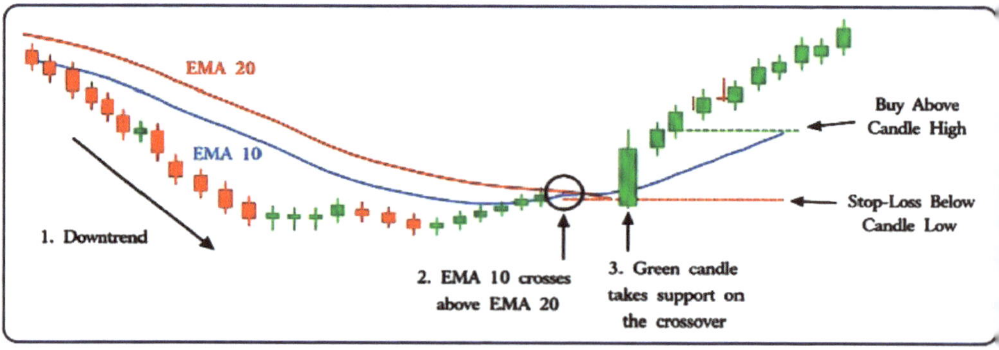

23 EMA + SUPER TREND SWING STRATEGY

Time Frame: 1 Day

Type: Swing

Indicators Used: 23 EMA, Supertrend (10, 3)

Indicator Settings

- 23 EMA
- Supertrend (10, 3)

Strategy Overview

This strategy is designed to capture strong bullish swing moves. It uses Supertrend to confirm trend direction and 23 EMA to identify overall trend bias. Enter only after Supertrend turns green following at least 2 weeks of red, and after price breaks a 5-candle resistance structure with strength.

Setup

1. Apply 23 EMA (close) on the daily chart.
2. Apply Supertrend (10, 3) on the daily chart.
3. Make sure Supertrend has been red for at least 2 weeks.
4. Wait for Supertrend to turn green.
5. After Supertrend turns green, wait for 5 daily candles to form.
6. Draw a horizontal resistance line at the highest high of those 5 candles.
7. All 5 candles must be above the 23 EMA.

Entry Rule

Enter a buy order above the high of the resistance candle (breakout candle) when price closes above the resistance line.

Stop-Loss

Place stop-loss below the low of the breakout candle.

Target

Hold the position until Supertrend turns red.

Trade Logic

Supertrend turning green after a prolonged red phase indicates a potential trend reversal. Waiting for 5 candles above the 23 EMA builds structure and filters out false signals. A breakout above the 5-candle high confirms buying strength. Stay in the trade as long as Supertrend remains green, even if price dips below the 23 EMA. Do not exit early, let the trend play out until Supertrend turns red.

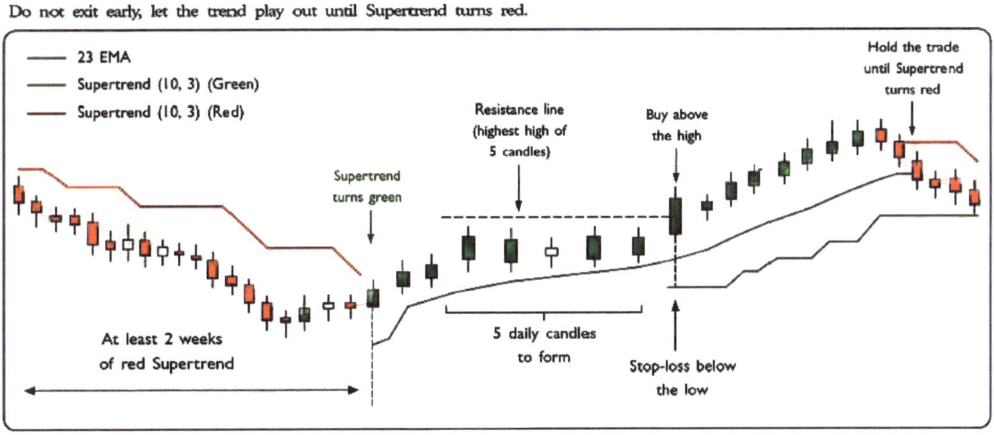

TRIPLE EMA + MACD SWING TRADING STRATEGY

Type: Swing

Time Frame: 1 Day, 15 Min

(1 Day time frame to find the stock and 15 Min for confirmation and buy)

Indicators Used:

Indicator	Length
EMA	5
EMA	15
EMA	45
MACD	(12, 26, 9)

These EMA's or Triple EMA (EMA 5, 15 and 45)

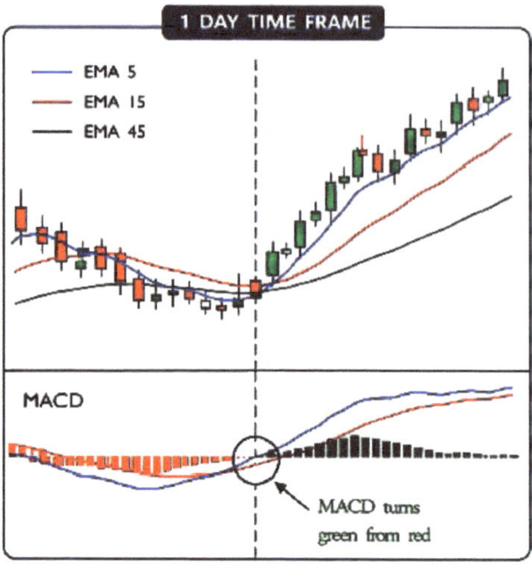

Draw vertical line exactly where MACD turns green from red

Strategy Overview

This strategy uses Triple EMA and MACD to find strong trending stocks on the 1 Day chart. Once MACD turns green from red, we move to the 15 Min chart to find a high-probability entry.

We enter when a green candle takes support on EMA 5 and EMA 15, and price is above the high of that candle.

We hold the trade until any candle takes support on or crosses the EMA 45 on the 15 Min chart.

Rules

1. **Stock Selection (1 Day Time Frame)**

- Add EMA 5, EMA 15, EMA 45 and MACD on the 1 Day chart.
- Wait for MACD to turn green from red.
- The day MACD turns green, draw a vertical line on the chart.
- This is your signal day.

2. **Entry (15 Min Time Frame)**

- Change the time frame to 15 minutes.
- Locate the vertical line on the 15 Min chart.
- After the vertical line, wait for a green candle that:
  - **Takes support on EMA 5 and EMA 15**
  - Is above the high of that candle.
- Buy above the high of that candle.
- Stop-loss: Below the low of that candle.

3. **Exit**

- Hold the trade until any candle takes support on or crosses the EMA 45 (15 Min chart).

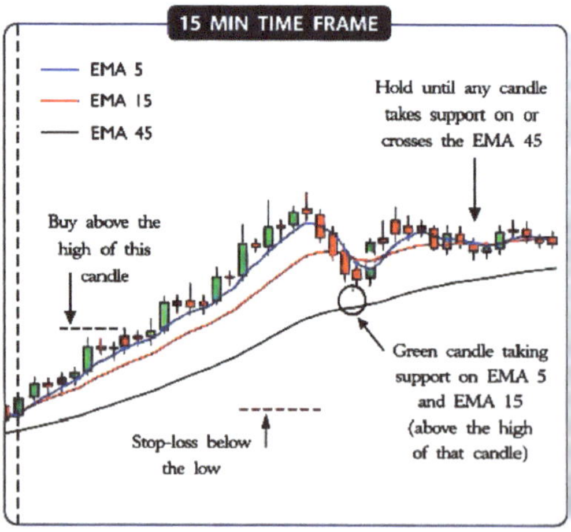

STRATEGY FLOW

1 Day Chart MACD turns green from red Draw vertical line → **Switch to 15 Min Chart** Find the vertical line → Wait for green candle taking support on EMA 5 & EMA 15 and above the high → **Buy above the high** Stop-loss below the low → Hold the trade until any candle takes support on or crosses EMA 45

QUANT TRADING STRATEGY

Time Frame: 1 Day
Type: Swing
Indicators Used:

- EMA 10
- Supertrend
- MACD

Indicator Settings

EMA 10 : Length 10
Supertrend : Default Settings
MACD : Default Settings

Strategy Overview

This strategy is designed to identify strong swing trading opportunities by combining trend confirmation from the Supertrend, dynamic support from the 10 EMA, and momentum confirmation using MACD.
It focuses on entering established trends instead of predicting reversals.

Setup

1. Open the Daily Time Frame.
2. Apply EMA 10, Supertrend, and MACD.
3. Select stocks where the Supertrend has recently turned green.
4. Wait for a green candle to take support on the 10 EMA.
5. Confirm that the MACD histogram is green at the same time.

Entry Rule

Buy above the high of the green support candle after all conditions are satisfied.

Stop-Loss

Place the stop-loss below the low of the entry candle.

Target

Ride the trend until your preferred exit method or risk management rule is triggered.

Trade Logic

A recently green Supertrend confirms an established bullish trend.
A green candle taking support on the 10 EMA indicates buyers are defending the trend, while a green MACD confirms bullish momentum. When all three conditions align, the probability of a successful swing trade increases.

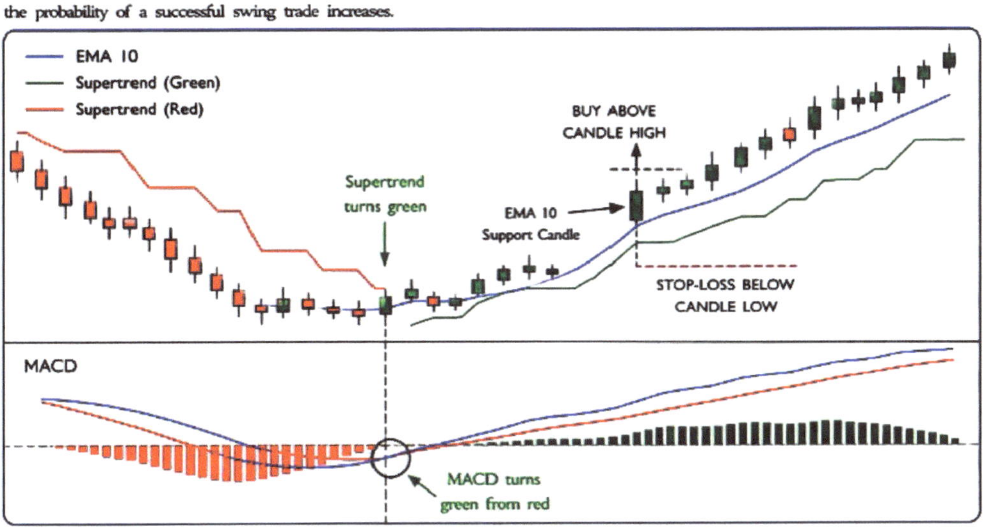

Choosing the Right Time Frame

Time Frame: Any (depending on trading style)

Type: Concept

Overview:

Selecting the right time frame is important for accurate analysis and better trading decisions. Different time frames serve different purposes and suit different trading styles.

Factors to Consider:

1. Your trading style (scalping, day trading, swing trading, long-term investing)
2. The amount of time you can dedicate to trading
3. The level of noise you can tolerate
4. Your risk tolerance

Guidelines:

- Lower time frames show more detail but contain more noise.
- Higher time frames show the bigger picture and are less noisy.
- Always align your analysis with your trading goal.

Popular Time Frames:

- Scalping: 1 min, 3 min, 5 min, 15 min
- Day Trading: 15 min, 30 min, 1 hour
- Swing Trading: 4 hour, Daily
- Long-Term Investing: Weekly, Monthly

Trade Logic:

Use higher time frames to identify the trend and key levels. Then, use lower time frames to find precise entry and exit points in the direction of the trend.

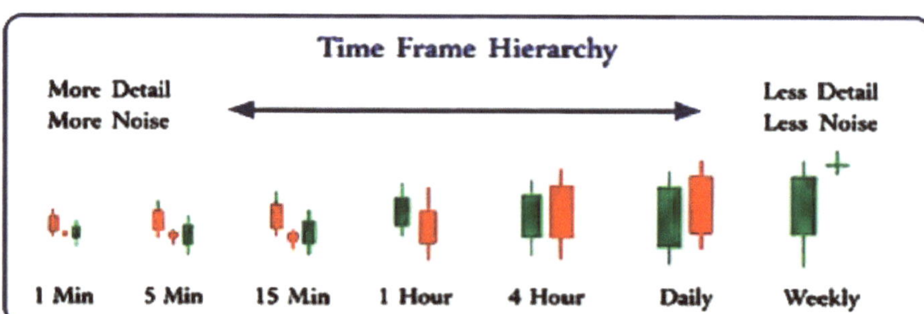

CHAPTER SUMMARY

Key Takeaways:

1. Elliott Wave Theory helps in understanding market psychology and predicting future price movements.
2. Markets move in 5 impulse waves and 3 corrective waves.
3. Trends move in the direction of the impulse waves.
4. Corrections move against the trend and retrace a portion of the previous move.
5. RSI and EMA are powerful tools to confirm trend direction and potential reversals.
6. Candlestick patterns provide information about price action and market sentiment.
7. Combining price action, indicators, and proper risk management increases the probability of success.

Remember:

No strategy is 100% accurate. Consistency, discipline, and risk management are the keys to long-term success in trading.

Best Practices:

- Always trade with a plan.
- Use proper position sizing.
- Manage risk on every trade.
- Keep emotions out of trading.
- Review and learn from your trades.

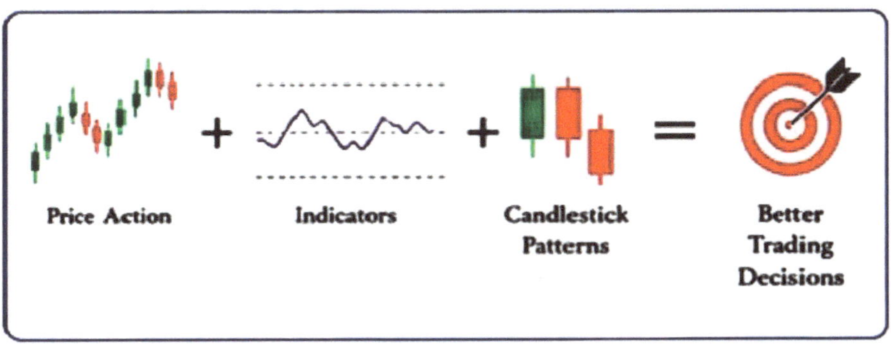

Chapter Summary (Continued)

Common Mistakes to Avoid:

1. Trading against the trend
2. Ignoring higher time frame trend
3. Overtrading
4. Not using stop-loss
5. Risking too much on a single trade
6. Expecting 100% accuracy
7. Letting emotions control decisions

Trading Checklist:

- Is the trend clear on higher time frame?
- Is the setup aligned with the trend?
- Do I have a valid entry signal?
- Is my stop-loss in place?
- Is my risk-reward ratio acceptable?
- Am I ready to accept any outcome?

Risk Management Rules:

- Never risk more than 1–2% of your capital on a single trade.
- Always use stop-loss.
- Protect your capital first; profits will follow.
- Survive today to trade tomorrow.

Practice & Patience:

The more you practice, the better you will get.
Patience and consistency are more important than winning every trade.

Risk Management Pyramid

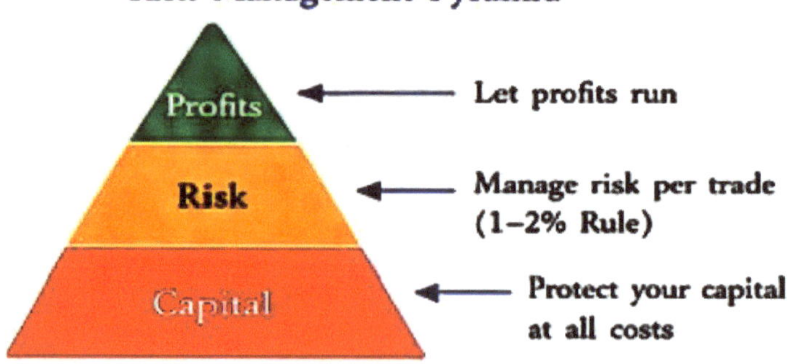

FINAL THOUGHTS

Trading is a Journey:

Trading is not a get-rich-quick scheme. It is a journey of learning, practicing, and growing. Every trader faces challenges, but those who stay committed and keep improving will achieve success.

Stay Focused on the Process:

- Focus on following your strategy.
- Focus on managing risk.
- Focus on continuous learning.
- Results will come with time.

Keep a Trading Journal:

Record your trades, thoughts, and emotions. Review them regularly to find your strengths and weaknesses.

Be Patient and Disciplined:

Patience helps you wait for the best setups.
Discipline helps you follow your plan and rules.

Believe in Yourself:

With the right knowledge, proper risk management,
and consistent effort, you can achieve your trading goals.
Stay positive, stay disciplined, and enjoy the journey!

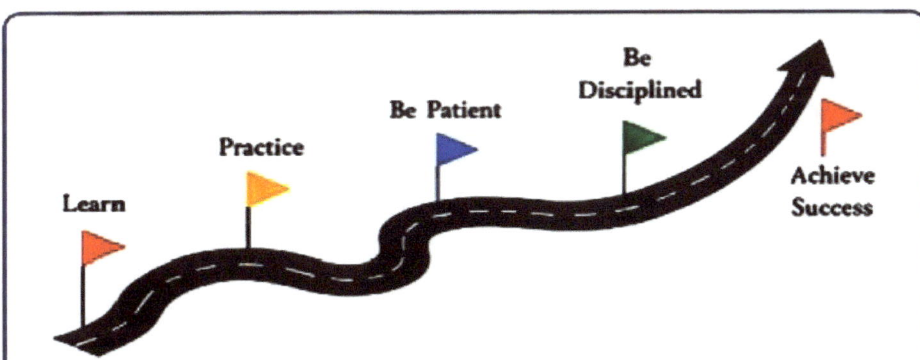

Chapter 10 Backtesting and Paper Trading

Introduction:

A great trading strategy is proven, not guessed. Before risking real money, every trader should test their strategy and gain experience in a risk-free environment.

In this chapter, you will learn about backtesting and paper trading—two powerful methods to test, validate, and refine your strategy. These steps help you build confidence and improve consistency before entering the real market.

Test your strategy. Learn from the results. Improve every day. That's how successful traders grow.

What You Will Learn:

- What backtesting is and how it works
- What paper trading is and why it's important
- How to use both methods to improve your strategy
- Best practices for getting the most out of testing

Why It Matters:

- Helps you avoid costly mistakes
- Builds confidence in your strategy
- Prepares you for real market conditions
- Improves your chances of long-term succes

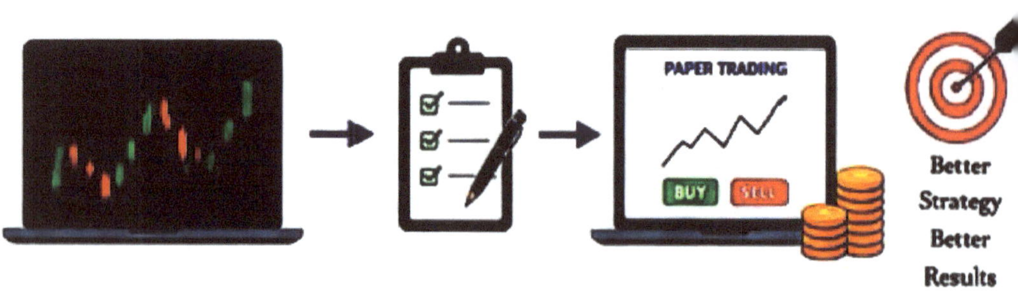

Backtesting

Backtesting means testing your trading strategy on historical data to see how it would have performed in the past.

Why Backtest?

- It shows if your strategy has an edge.
- It helps you find strengths and weaknesses.
- It builds confidence before real trading.

How to Backtest?

1. Choose a strategy to test.
2. Collect historical data.
3. Apply your strategy rules on the data.
4. Record all trades and results.
5. Analyze the performance.

What to Check in Backtesting?

- Win rate
- Risk to reward ratio
- Maximum drawdown
- Profit factor
- Consistency of results

Paper Trading

Paper trading means trading in a real market environment without using real money.

Why Paper Trade?

- It helps you practice without risk.
- It builds experience and discipline.
- It prepares you for real trading.

How to Paper Trade?

1. Choose a reliable platform.
2. Use real market data.
3. Trade as if it's real.
4. Follow your strategy rules strictly.
5. Review your trades and results.

What to Focus On?

- Following your plan
- Managing risk
- Controlling emotions
- Improving execution

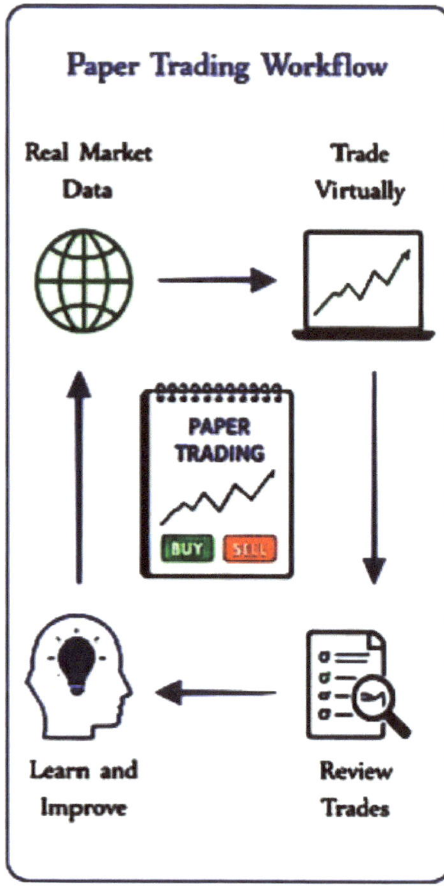

Comparing Backtesting vs Paper Trading

Both backtesting and paper trading are important,
but they serve different purposes.

Feature	Backtesting	Paper Trading
Data Used	Historical data	Live market data
Purpose	Test strategy in the past	Practice strategy in real time
Environment	Not real-time	Real-time
Emotions Involved	No	Yes
Best For	Strategy validation	Skill building and execution
Limitation	May not reflect real market	No real money involved

How to Use Both Together?

Backtest your strategy first.

Then paper trade to build confidence.

Make improvements based on both results.

Finally, trade with small real money.

The Improvement Cycle

Backtesting Metrics

Metrics help you measure how well your strategy performed in the past. They show the true quality of your edge.

1. **Win Rate**
   The percentage of winning trades.
   A higher win rate means your strategy wins more often.

2. **Risk-Reward Ratio**
   The average profit you make compared to the average loss you take.
   Aim for at least 1:1.5 or better.

3. **Profit Factor**
   Total gross profit divided by total gross loss.
   A profit factor above 1 means your strategy is profitable.

4. **Maximum Drawdown**
   The biggest drop from a peak to a trough in your equity curve.
   Lower drawdown means lower risk.

5. **Expectancy**
   The average amount you can expect to win or lose per trade.
   Positive expectancy = long-term edge.

Common Mistakes in Backtesting

- Using too little historical data
- Curve fitting (over-optimizing the strategy)
- Ignoring realistic conditions like slippage & fees
- Not testing across different market conditions
- Focusing only on win rate instead of all metrics

Remember:

A good strategy is not about high win rate. It's about having positive expectancy and managing risk consistently.

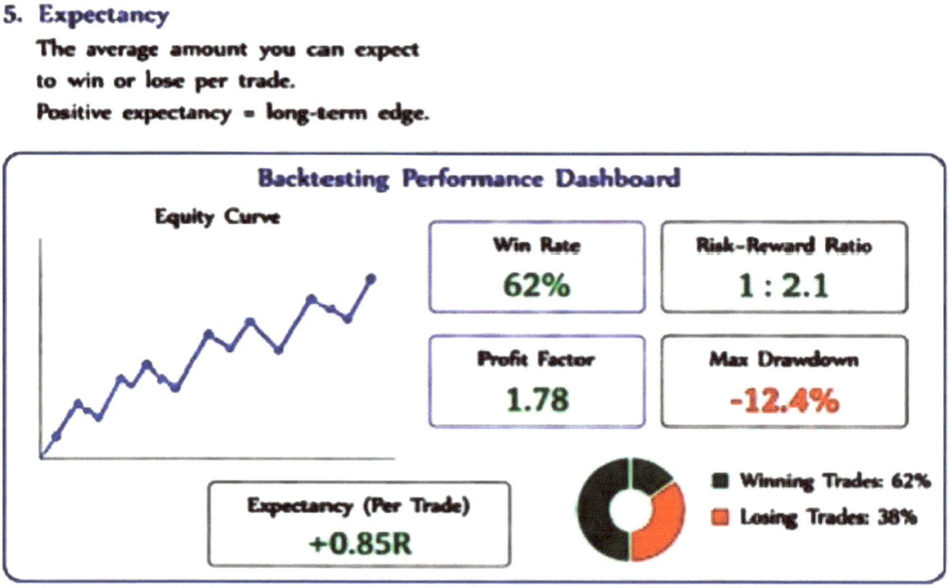

Paper Trading in Practice

Paper trading lets you practice in real market conditions without risking real money. Treat it like real trading.

1. Setting Up a Demo Account

- Choose a reliable broker that offers a demo account.
- Use the same platform and tools you will use for real trading.
- Start with virtual balance you would use in real trading.

2. Follow Your Trading Rules

- Use the same strategy you backtested.
- Follow your entry, exit, and risk management rules strictly.
- Do not change rules frequently.

3. Record Every Trade

- Log every trade in your journal.
- Note entry, exit, reason, size, and emotions.
- Review your trades regularly.

4. Avoid Emotional Decisions

- Treat paper trading seriously.
- Avoid revenge trading and overtrading.
- Focus on process, not profit.

Benefits of Paper Trading

- Builds confidence
- Helps you master your strategy
- Teaches patience and discipline
- Prepares you for real market conditions

Remember:

Paper trading is a training ground. The more seriously you practice, the better you will perform in real trading.

TRADING JOURNAL

A trading journal is your best teacher. It helps you track, learn, and improve every day.

1. Why Every Trader Needs One

- Helps you identify strengths and weaknesses.
- Shows patterns in your behavior and results.
- Keeps you accountable.
- Helps you avoid repeating the same mistakes.

2. What to Record

- Date and time
- Market / Asset
- Setup / Strategy
- Entry and Exit points
- Position size
- Reason for the trade
- Result (Win/Loss)
- Emotions during the trade
- Lessons learned

3. Sample Journal Fields

Date	12 May 2025
Asset	EUR/USD
Time Frame	1 Hour
Setup	Breakout
Entry	1.0850
Exit	1.0910
Position Size	1% of capital
Result	Win (+60 pips)
Reason	Breakout above resistance with volume
Emotions	Calm and confident
Lesson	Waited for confirmation. Good discipline.

4. Reviewing Mistakes

- Review your losing trades regularly.
- Identify the reason for the loss.
- Write down the lesson.
- Focus on improvement, not perfection.

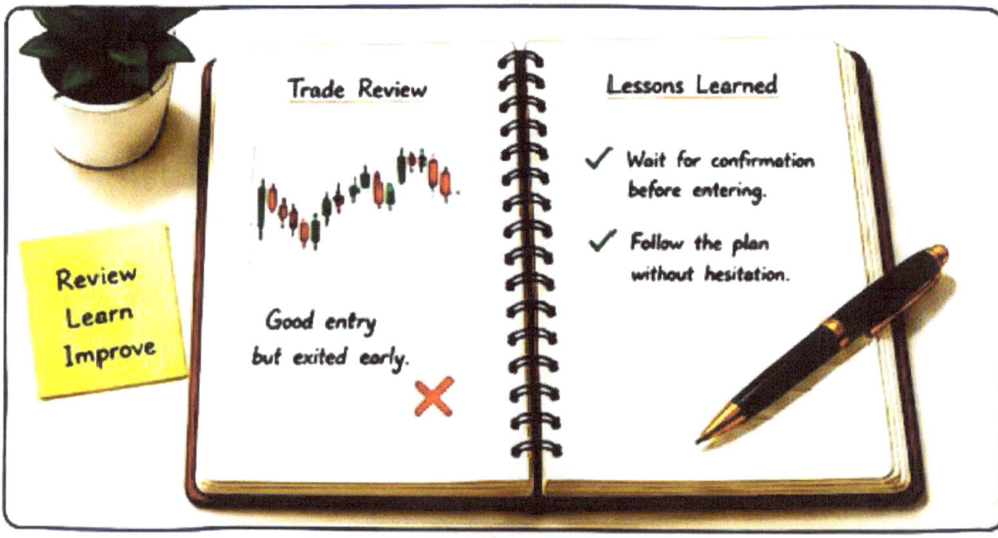

Combining Everything

Backtesting and paper trading work together. Use them in sequence to build a strong and consistent strategy.

1. The Complete Workflow

1. Learn
Learn technical analysis, price action, and strategy concepts.

↓

2. Backtest
Test your strategy on historical data and analyze the results.

↓

3. Paper Trade
Practice your strategy in real market conditions without risk.

↓

4. Improve
Review your performance, fix mistakes, and refine your strategy.

↓

5. Live Trading
Trade with real money with confidence and proper risk management.

2. Key Takeaways

- Test before you risk real money.
- Backtesting shows potential.
- Paper trading builds confidence.
- Consistency comes from the process.
- Risk management is the key to survival.

Remember:

The goal is not to get rich quick. The goal is to be consistent and profitable over the long term. Build the right process, and the results will follow.

What's Next?

Now that you know how to test and improve your strategy, the next step is to manage your trades like a professional. The next chapter will teach you all about **Risk Management.**

Consistency + Discipline + Patience = Long-Term Success

Avoiding Common Pitfalls in Testing

Even with the best tools, many traders make mistakes during backtesting and paper trading. Avoiding these pitfalls will help you get accurate results and become a better trader.

1. **Overfitting Your Strategy**
   Making a strategy too complex for past data can lead to poor future performance. Keep it simple and realistic.

2. **Using Too Little Data**
   Testing on a small amount of data may not show how the strategy performs in different market conditions.

3. **Ignoring Transaction Costs**
   Commissions, spreads, and slippage can reduce profits. Always include costs in your backtests.

4. **Not Considering Market Conditions**
   Markets change. Test your strategy in trending, ranging, and volatile conditions.

5. **Breaking Your Own Rules**
   Changing rules during testing or paper trading leads to inconsistent results. Stick to your plan.

6. **Overtrading in Paper Trading**
   Trading too often in a demo account can create bad habits and false confidence.

7. **Not Reviewing Results**
   If you don't review your trades, you will repeat the same mistakes again and again.

Remember:
Discipline in testing leads to clarity in strategy and confidence in execution.

Advanced Backtesting Tips

Once you understand the basics, use these advanced tips to perform high-quality backtests and gain deeper insights.

1. Use Multiple Time Frames

- Test your strategy on different time frames.
- It helps you see how the strategy performs in various market environments.

2. Perform Out-of-Sample Testing

- Test on data that was not used in developing the strategy.
- It shows how well your strategy works in new conditions.

3. Walk-Forward Analysis

- Test your strategy in a moving window.
- It mimics real market conditions and reduces overfitting.

4. Monte Carlo Simulation

- Randomly change the order of trades.
- It helps you understand the potential range of outcomes.

5. Stress Testing

- Test your strategy during extreme market events.
- It prepares you for worst-case scenarios.

Key Benefit:

Advanced testing gives you a realistic view of your strategy's strength and weaknesses.

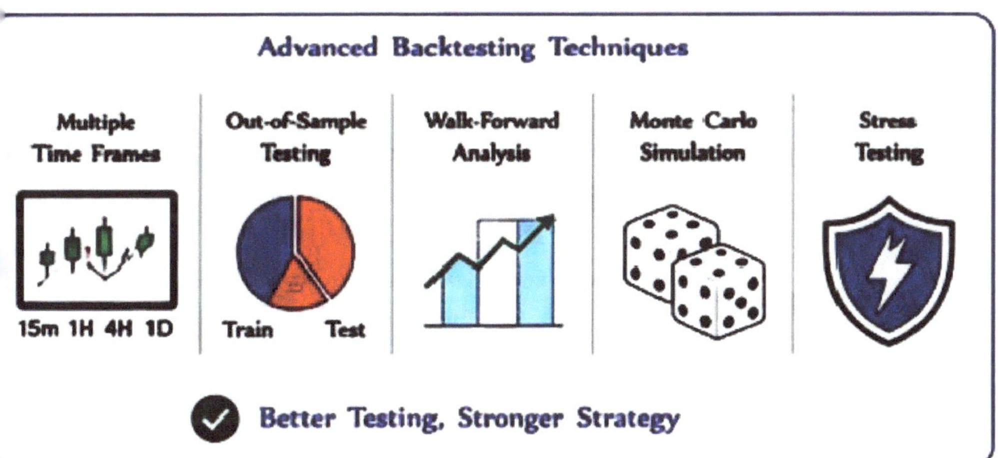

From Paper Trading to Live Trading

Paper trading prepares you for real trading, but the transition needs careful planning. Here's how to make the shift successfully.

1. Build Consistent Results

- Achieve consistent profits in paper trading.
- Don't move to live trading too early.

2. Start Small

- Begin with a small amount of real money.
- Small risk builds confidence.

3. Keep the Same Rules

- Use the same strategy and risk management.
- Do not change your plan.

4. Manage Emotions

- Real money brings real emotions.
- Stay calm, patient, and disciplined.

5. Review and Adjust

- Review your trades regularly.
- Adjust only if your strategy needs improvement.

Remember:

The goal is not to get rich quick. The goal is to be consistent and grow steadily.

A Smooth Transition

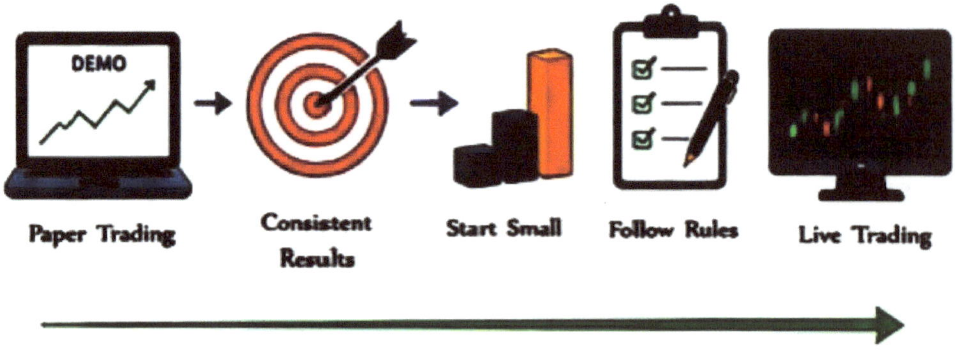

Patience Today, Profits Tomorrow

Building a Testing Routine

A good routine makes testing more effective and helps you improve faster. Follow this simple routine every week.

1. Plan

- Define what you will test.
- Set clear goals for the week.

2. Backtest

- Test your strategy on historical data.
- Analyze the results.

3. Paper Trade

- Practice your strategy in real market conditions.
- Record every trade.

4. Review

- Review your trades and results.
- Find mistakes and strengths.

5. Improve

- Make improvements to your strategy or execution.
- Prepare for the next week.

Key Point:

Consistency in your routine creates long-term success in trading.

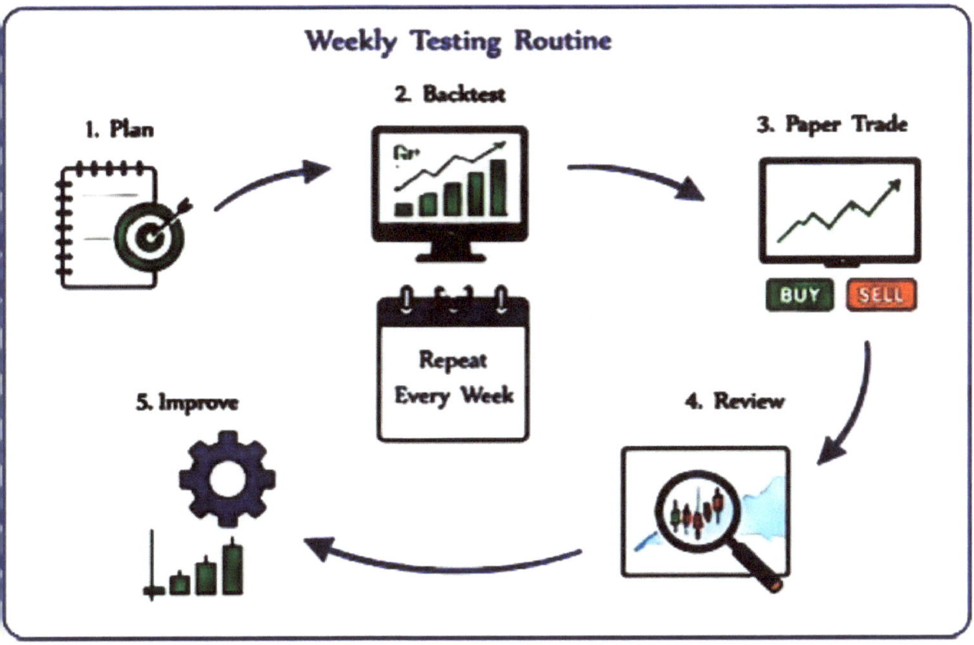

Performance Analysis & Trade Statistics

Analyzing your results helps you understand what is working, what is not, and how to improve your edge.

1. Win Rate

- Shows the percentage of winning trades.
- A good win rate depends on your strategy and risk-reward.
- Quality of trades matters more than quantity.

2. Expectancy (Per Trade)

- Measures the average amount you can expect to win or lose per trade.
- Positive expectancy = long-term profitability.
- Formula:

> Expectancy = (Win Rate × Avg Win) − (Loss Rate × Avg Loss)

3. Drawdown Analysis

- Drawdown shows the biggest decline from a peak in your equity curve.
- Smaller drawdowns mean better risk control.
- Learn from periods of high drawdown.

4. Other Important Stats

- Profit Factor: Gross Profit / Gross Loss
- Average Win: Average profit of winning trades
- Average Loss: Average loss of losing trades
- Trade Count: Total number of trades
- Payoff Ratio: Avg Win / Avg Loss

Remember:

Numbers don't lie. Let your statistics guide your decisions, not emotions. Focus on improving your process, and the profits will follow.

Sample Performance Report

Total Trades	120
Winning Trades	72 (60%)
Losing Trades	48 (40%)
Win Rate	60%
Profit Factor	2.15
Expectancy (Per Trade)	+0.85R
Average Win	+1.35R
Average Loss	-0.81R
Max Drawdown	-14.2%

Equity Curve

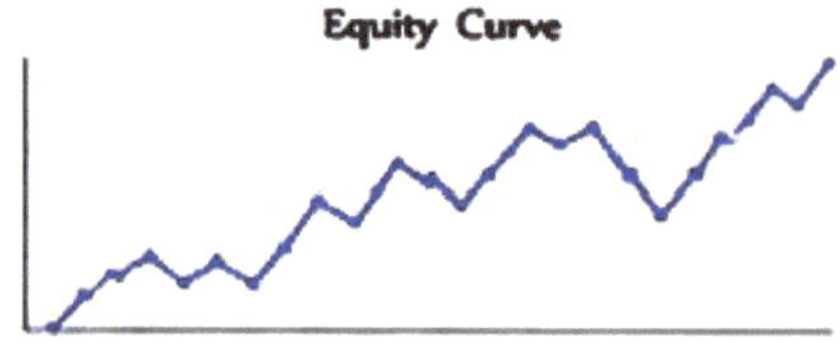

Drawdown Chart

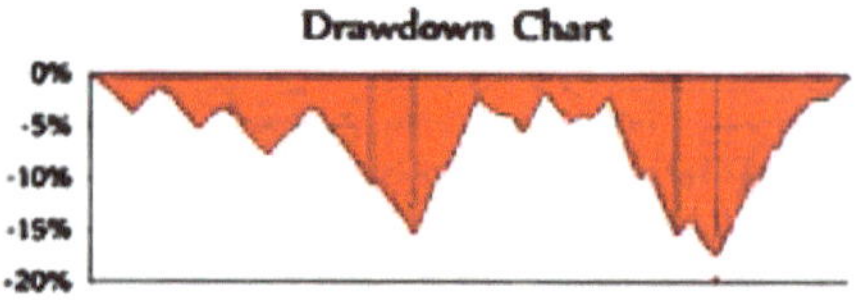

Creating a Professional Trading Plan

A trading plan keeps you focused and removes guesswork.
Write it down, follow it, and review it regularly.

1. Entry Rules

- Define exact conditions to enter a trade.
- Include indicators, price action, or patterns.
- Be specific and avoid confusion.

2. Exit Rules

- Define profit targets.
- Define stop-loss placement.
- Use trailing stops if your strategy allows.
- Know when to take partial profits.

3. Risk Management

- Risk a fixed percentage per trade (e.g., 1–2% of capital).
- Never risk more than planned.
- Protect your capital at all times.

4. Position Sizing

- Calculate position size based on your risk and stop-loss.
- Use this formula:

$$\text{Position Size} = \frac{\text{Risk Amount}}{\text{Stop Loss (in pips or \$)}}$$

5. Trading Checklist

- Is the setup valid?
- Is the risk within limit?
- Is the trend clear?
- Is my mind clear and focused?
- Am I following my plan?

Remember:

A good plan won't make you rich quick, but a bad plan will make you poor quickly.

Trading Plan Blueprint

Entry Rules	Exit Rules	Risk Management	Position Sizing	Checklist

When to enter the trade	When and how to exit	Protect your capital	Calculate the right size	Follow every time

Chapter Summary

Backtesting and paper trading are powerful tools that help you build a strong foundation for real trading success.

1. Key Takeaways

- Backtesting helps you test and validate your strategy using historical data.
- Paper trading helps you practice in real market conditions without risking money.
- Both methods build confidence, discipline, and consistency.
- Proper analysis and a trading plan improve your performance.

2. Common Mistakes

- Ignoring risk management
- Backtesting with poor quality data
- Over-optimizing strategies
- Not following rules in paper trading
- Letting emotions control decisions

3. Best Practices

- Test your strategy on different market conditions.
- Follow your trading plan strictly.
- Keep a trading journal and review regularly.
- Focus on long-term results, not short-term gains.
- Stay patient, consistent, and disciplined.

The Path to Consistent Trading

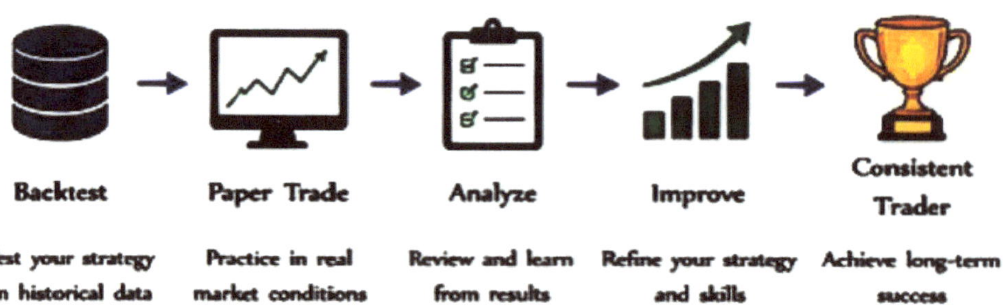

FINAL THOUGHTS

Backtesting and paper trading are essential steps that separate prepared traders from hopeful ones. They allow you to test your strategy, refine your approach, and build the confidence needed before risking real capital.

Keep learning, stay disciplined, and trust the process. The market rewards those who prepare patiently, adapt consistently, and manage risk wisely. Every great trader was once a student who refused to skip these important steps.

> The secret to trading success is not in being right every time, but in managing risk every time.
>
> — Van K. Tharp

CHAPTER 11

BUILDING YOUR TRADING PLAN

A trading plan is your roadmap to consistent success. It defines your strategy, rules, and risk management approach before you enter the market. Without a plan, emotions take over. With a plan, you trade with clarity, discipline, and purpose.

This chapter will guide you through creating a complete trading plan that fits your personality, goals, and lifestyle. Your plan is not just a document—it's your commitment to becoming a professional trader.

Components of a Trading Plan

A strong trading plan has several key components that work together to keep you focused and disciplined.

1. Trading Goals

- Define your short-term and long-term goals.
- Be specific, measurable, and realistic.

2. Trading Strategy

- Describe your strategy in detail.
- Include the markets, timeframes, and tools you use.

3. Entry & Exit Rules

- Define clear criteria for entering a trade.
- Define rules for taking profit and cutting loss.

4. Risk Management

- Set your risk per trade.
- Define stop-loss rules and maximum drawdown.

5. Position Sizing

- Determine how much to risk on each trade.
- Use a consistent position sizing method.

6. Trade Management

- Define how to manage open trades.
- Include scaling, trailing stops, and adjustments.

7. Review & Improvement

- Review your trades and performance regularly.
- Continuously refine your plan.

SETTING ENTRY & EXIT RULES

Clear entry and exit rules remove hesitation and keep emotions out of your decisions. Your rules should be based on your strategy and market conditions.

1. Entry Rules

- Define the exact conditions you need for a valid setup.
- Use indicators, price action, or patterns.
- Wait for confirmation before entering.

Example Entry Rule

Enter a long trade when:

✓ Price is above 50 EMA

✓ RSI is above 50

✓ Bullish candlestick pattern forms at support

2. Exit Rules

- Define your profit target.
- Define your stop-loss level.
- Consider a trailing stop for trend trades.

Example Exit Rule

Exit the trade when:

✓ Price reaches 2R profit

✓ Or hit stop-loss at 1R

✓ Or trend shows weakness

Types of Exits

Fixed Target
Set a specific profit target based on risk-reward.

Trailing Stop
Lock in profits while giving the trade room to run.

Manual Exit
Exit based on market conditions or strategy rules.

Risk Management Rules

Risk management is the most important part of your trading plan. Protect your capital so you can stay in the game long enough to win.

1. Risk Per Trade

- Risk a small percentage of your account on each trade.
- Recommended: 1% - 2%.

Risk Per Trade Formula

Risk Per Trade = Account Size × Risk %

Example:

Account Size = $10,000

Risk % = 1%

Risk Per Trade = $10,000 × 1% = $100

2. Maximum Daily Loss

- Limit your daily loss to protect your capital and mindset.
- Recommended: 3% - 5% of your account.

Stay in the Green Zone

3. Maximum Drawdown

- Set a maximum drawdown limit.
- If reached, stop trading and review your plan.
- Recommended: 10% - 20%.

Example

If your max drawdown is 15% and your account is $10,000, you stop trading if equity falls to $8,500.

4. Risk Management Checklist

- ☑ I risk only 1% - 2% per trade.
- ☑ I use stop-loss on every trade.
- ☑ I follow my position sizing rules.
- ☑ I avoid overtrading.
- ☑ I stop trading after hitting my daily loss limit.
- ☑ I protect my capital at all times.

Backtesting Metrics

Metrics help you measure how well your strategy performed in the past. They show the true quality of your edge.

1. **Win Rate**
   The percentage of winning trades.
   A higher win rate means your strategy wins more often.

2. **Risk-Reward Ratio**
   The average profit you make compared to the average loss you take.
   Aim for at least 1:1.5 or better.

3. **Profit Factor**
   Total gross profit divided by total gross loss.
   A profit factor above 1 means your strategy is profitable.

4. **Maximum Drawdown**
   The biggest drop from a peak to a trough in your equity curve.
   Lower drawdown means lower risk.

5. **Expectancy**
   The average amount you can expect to win or lose per trade.
   Positive expectancy = long-term edge.

Common Mistakes in Backtesting

- Using too little historical data
- Curve fitting (over-optimizing the strategy)
- Ignoring realistic conditions like slippage & fees
- Not testing across different market conditions
- Focusing only on win rate instead of all metrics

Remember:

A good strategy is not about high win rate. It's about having positive expectancy and managing risk consistently.

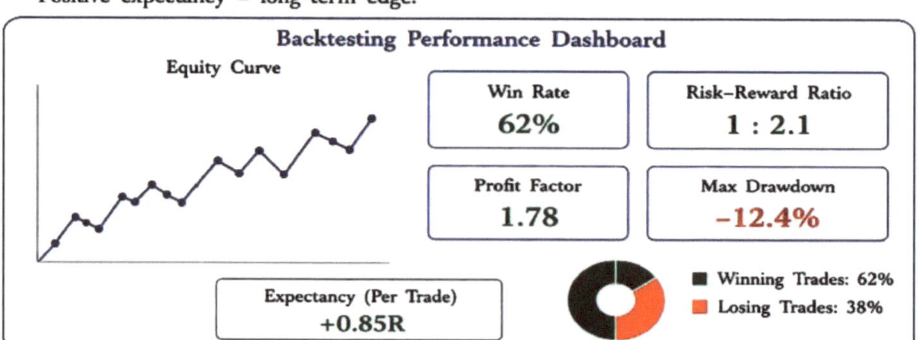

Paper Trading in Practice

Paper trading lets you practice in real market conditions without risking real money. Treat it like real trading.

1. Setting Up a Demo Account

- Choose a reliable broker that offers a demo account.
- Use the same platform and tools you will use for real trading.
- Start with virtual balance you would use in real trading.

2. Follow Your Trading Rules

- Use the same strategy you backtested.
- Follow your entry, exit, and risk management rules strictly.
- Do not change rules frequently.

3. Record Every Trade

- Log every trade in your journal.
- Note entry, exit, reason, size, and emotions.
- Review your trades regularly.

4. Avoid Emotional Decisions

- Treat paper trading seriously.
- Avoid revenge trading and overtrading.
- Focus on process, not profit.

Benefits of Paper Trading

- Builds confidence
- Helps you master your strategy
- Teaches patience and discipline
- Prepares you for real market conditions

Remember:

Paper trading is a training ground. The more seriously you practice, the better you will perform in real trading.

TRADING GOALS

Clear goals give your trading direction, motivation, and purpose. They help you stay focused and measure your progress over time.

1. SHORT-TERM GOALS (1–3 MONTHS)

- Build consistency in following your plan.
- Improve win rate and risk management.
- Track every trade and maintain a journal.

2. MEDIUM-TERM GOALS (3–12 MONTHS)

- Achieve steady monthly returns.
- Improve strategy performance.
- Reduce mistakes and emotional trades.

3. LONG-TERM GOALS (1 YEAR AND BEYOND)

- Become a consistently profitable trader.
- Grow capital significantly.
- Achieve financial freedom through trading.

4. SMART GOALS FRAMEWORK

S Specific
M Achievable
A Time-bound

- Measurable
- Relevant

EXAMPLE GOAL SHEET

My 3-Month Goal

Become consistent and achieve 5% monthly return.

Target Date: 30 Sep 2025

My 6-Month Goal

Improve win rate to 60% and reduce average loss.

Target Date: 31 Dec 2025

My 1-Year Goal

Generate 15% average monthly return consistently.

Target Date: 30 Jun 2026

KEY REMINDERS

- ☑ Write down your goals.
- ☑ Review them weekly.
- ☑ Stay patient and consistent.
- ☑ Focus on the process, not results.

Trading Journal & Record Keeping

A trading journal is your mirror. It shows you your strengths, weaknesses, and areas to improve. Successful traders keep records of every trade.

Why Keep a Trading Journal?

- ☑ Helps identify strengths and weaknesses.
- ☑ Reveals repeating mistakes.
- ☑ Improves discipline and consistency.
- ☑ Tracks long-term progress.

What to Record

- Date & Time
- Market / Asset
- Timeframe
- Strategy Used
- Entry Price
- Stop-Loss
- Take-Profit
- Position Size
- Risk %
- Result (Profit/Loss)
- Screenshot of Chart
- Emotions During Trade
- Lessons Learned
- Notes

Example Trade Record

Date	15 May 2025
Market	EUR/USD
Timeframe	1H
Setup	Bullish Breakout
Entry	1.0850
Exit	1.0915
Stop-Loss	1.0815
Take-Profit	1.0950
Risk	1%
Result	+65 Pips (+0.60%)
Notes	Good breakout, waited for confirmation.
Emotions	Calm and focused.
Lesson	Patience before entry paid off.

Benefits

- Builds consistency
- Improves decision making
- Makes performance measurable
- Helps refine your trading plan

Daily & Weekly Trading Routine

A good routine builds discipline and consistency. Follow a structured process before, during, and after the market.

1. Pre-Market
(Before the Market Opens)

- Check economic calendar and news.
- Analyze market trends and key levels.
- Review watchlist and potential setups.
- Prepare trading plan for the day.

2. During Market
(While Trading)

- Follow your trading plan strictly.
- Wait for valid setups.
- Manage risk and emotions.
- Avoid overtrading.

3. Post-Market
(After Market Closes)

- Review all trades taken.
- Record in trading journal.
- Analyze mistakes and wins.
- Plan for the next trading day.

Weekly Trading Routine

1. Review weekly performance.
2. Analyze winning and losing trades.
3. Identify mistakes and their reasons.
4. Adjust strategy if needed.
5. Set goals for the upcoming week.

Example Weekly Review Sheet

Total Trades	25
Winning Trades	15
Losing Trades	10
Win Rate	60%
Total Profit	+$850
Total Loss	–$450
Net Result	+$400
Lessons Learned	Wait for confirmation.

Key Reminders

✓ Follow your routine every day.
✓ Consistency in routine = Consistency in results.
✓ Small daily improvements lead to big long-term success.

Common Mistakes in Planning

Avoiding mistakes is just as important as having a good plan. Many traders fail because they ignore these common errors.

1. No Clear Plan

Trading without a plan leads to confusion and emotional decisions.

Solution:
Always trade with a written plan.

2. Overcomplicating the Plan

Using too many indicators and rules creates confusion.

Solution:
Keep it simple and follow it strictly.

3. Ignoring Risk Management

Risking too much per trade can wipe out your account.

Solution:
Always risk only 1%–2% per trade.

4. Emotional Decisions

Fear, greed, and impulses lead to poor decisions.

Solution:
Control emotions and stick to your plan.

5. No Record Keeping

Not tracking trades prevents you from learning and improving.

Solution:
Maintain a trading journal.

6. Changing Strategy Too Often

Frequent changes prevent consistency and results.

Solution:
Give your strategy time to work.

7. Overtrading

Trading too much leads to more mistakes and higher losses.

Solution:
Trade quality setups, not quantity.

8. Unrealistic Expectations

Expecting quick riches leads to frustration and poor choices.

Solution:
Be patient and focus on long-term growth.

Key Takeaway

A good plan is your roadmap, but avoiding these mistakes keeps you on the right path.

Sample Professional Trading Plan

A trading plan keeps your decisions clear and consistent. Here is an example of a simple and effective trading plan.

1. Purpose

Why I trade.

- Achieve financial freedom.
- Build long-term consistent profits.
- Improve and grow every day.

2. Market

Where I trade.

- Forex market
- Major currency pairs
- 1H and 4H timeframes

3. Strategy

How I trade.

- Trend following strategy
- Support and resistance
- Price action confirmation
- Risk-reward minimum 1:2

4. Risk Management

How I protect my capital.

- Risk only 1%–2% per trade
- Use stop-loss on every trade
- No revenge trading
- Protect capital first

5. Trade Management

What I do in a trade.

- Move stop to break-even
- Take partial profits
- Let winners run

6. Review & Improvement

How I grow.

- Keep a trading journal
- Review trades weekly
- Learn from mistakes
- Keep improving

Trading Plan Checklist

Use this checklist to create and follow your trading plan. Review it regularly to stay on track.

1. Plan Foundation

- [ ] I know my purpose for trading.
- [ ] I have clear financial goals.
- [ ] I have a written trading plan.

2. Strategy & Setup

- [ ] I have a trading strategy.
- [ ] I know the markets and timeframes I trade.
- [ ] I have specific entry and exit rules.
- [ ] I have a risk-reward ratio of at least 1:2.

3. Risk Management

- [ ] I risk only 1%–2% per trade.
- [ ] I always use stop-loss.
- [ ] I never risk more than I can afford to lose.
- [ ] I avoid revenge trading.

4. Trade Management

- [ ] I have a plan for managing trades.
- [ ] I take partial profits.
- [ ] I let winners run with a plan.

5. Review & Improvement

- [ ] I keep a trading journal.
- [ ] I review my trades weekly.
- [ ] I learn from mistakes.
- [ ] I keep improving my skills and mindset.

Chapter Summary

This chapter covered the most important steps to build a strong trading plan. A good plan brings clarity, discipline, and consistency to your trading.

1. Set Your Goals

Clear goals give your trading direction and motivation. They help you stay focused and measure progress.

2. Keep a Trading Journal

A trading journal helps you identify strengths, weaknesses, and areas to improve.

3. Follow a Routine

A daily and weekly routine builds discipline and ensures you are always prepared.

4. Avoid Common Mistakes

Avoiding common mistakes saves money, time, and emotional stress.

5. Build and Follow Your Plan

A well-structured plan with risk management and review leads to long-term success.

Remember

A trading plan is not just a document.
It is your roadmap to becoming a successful trader.
Follow it, review it, and improve it.

Final Thought

A trading plan is the foundation of your trading success.
It keeps you focused, disciplined, and in control.
Without a plan, you are just guessing.
With a plan, you are trading with purpose.

Keep Building, Keep Growing

Your best trades are still ahead of you.
Stay committed to your plan, and the results will follow.

Chapter 12

Becoming a Consistent Trader

Consistency is the bridge between
knowledge and freedom.
It is built through discipline, patience,
and smart habits.
Every small step you take today
shapes the trader
you will become tomorrow.
The journey to consistency starts now!

What Consistency Really Means

Consistency is doing the right things repeatedly over time.
It is not about perfection.
A consistent trader focuses on what they can control.

1. Following Your Plan

Stick to your trading plan every time.
Do not make random decisions.

2. Managing Risk

Risk a small amount on every trade.
Protect your capital first.

3. Staying Disciplined

Control your emotions and avoid impulses.
Discipline creates freedom.

4. Keeping it Simple

Trade simple strategies you understand.
Simplicity leads to consistent results.

5. Continuous Improvement

Learn from every trade and keep getting better.
Small improvements create big results.

Key Takeaway

Consistency is a habit built on discipline,
patience, and a strong trading process.

Daily Habits of Successful Traders

Your daily habits shape your long-term results.
Great traders focus on these essential habits every day.

1. Prepare Before the Market

Analyze the market, check your watchlist, and plan your trades.

2. Follow Your Plan

Execute your trades exactly as planned.
No deviations, no excuses.

3. Keep a Trading Journal

Record every trade and review it.
Learn from your mistakes and wins.

4. Manage Your Mind & Body

Stay fit, eat well, and get enough sleep.
A healthy body supports a sharp mind.

5. Review & Improve

End your day by reviewing your trades.
Find ways to improve tomorrow.

Key Takeaway

Small daily habits lead to big long-term success.
Be consistent with your habits, and results will follow.

Developing Discipline & Patience

Discipline keeps you on track.
Patience keeps you in the game long enough to win.
Both are essential for long-term success.

1. Follow Rules, not Feelings

Your plan is more reliable than your emotions.
Trust your rules, not your impulses.

2. Wait for the Right Setups

Good trades come to those who wait.
Patience helps you avoid poor trades.

3. Focus on the Process

You can control your process, not the outcome.
Focus on what you can control.

4. Stay Committed

Discipline is doing what you should do,
even when you don't feel like it.

Key Takeaway

Discipline and patience compound over time.
They turn a good trader into a great one.

Managing Emotions Under Pressure

Emotions are normal, but letting them control your trades can be dangerous. The key is to understand and manage them. Stay calm, think clearly, and stick to your plan.

1. Recognize Your Emotions

Notice what you feel before, during, and after trades.
Awareness is the first step.

2. Stay Calm Under Pressure

Take deep breaths. Step away if needed.
A calm mind makes better decisions.

3. Don't Let Emotions Decide

Never let fear, greed, or anger control your actions.
Let your plan decide.

4. Take Breaks

When emotions run high, take a break.
Come back when your mind is clear.

5. Accept That Losses Happen

Losses are part of trading.
Accept them, learn from them, and move on.

Key Takeaway

Control your emotions, or your emotions will control your trading.

Learning From Every Trade

Every trade teaches you something valuable.
Winners build your confidence, but losers build your experience.
The goal is to learn, improve, and keep moving forward.

1. Review Every Trade

After each trade, review what you did well and what you could improve.

2. Focus on the Process

Don't just look at the result.
Evaluate your decisions and execution.

3. Look for Patterns

Find patterns in your wins and losses.
This helps you spot strengths and weaknesses.

4. Make Small Improvements

Improve 1% every day.
Small changes lead to big results over time.

5. Keep a Growth Mindset

See every trade as an opportunity to learn, not just to make money.

Key Takeaway

The best traders are lifelong students.
Learn from every trade and keep improving.

Creating a Growth Mindset

A growth mindset helps you see challenges as opportunities to learn and grow. It keeps you improving, even when things get tough.
Great traders never stop learning.

1. Embrace Challenges

Challenges make you stronger.
Face them with confidence and a positive attitude.

2. Learn from Mistakes

Mistakes are not failures, they are lessons.
Analyze, learn, and use them to improve.

3. Focus on Progress, not Perfection

Small, consistent progress leads to big results.
Aim to improve 1% each day.

4. Stay Curious

The more you learn, the more you earn.
Stay curious and keep exploring new ideas.

5. Believe in Yourself

Confidence comes from preparation and experience.
Believe in your ability to grow and succeed.

Key Takeaway

A growth mindset turns every experience into an opportunity to become a better trader.

Avoiding Common Trading Traps

Many traders struggle not because of their strategy, but because of bad habits. Avoid these common traps to protect your mindset and your account.

1. **Overtrading**
   Trading too much leads to mistakes and losses. Wait for the right setup.

2. **Revenge Trading**
   Trying to win back losses quickly leads to bigger losses. Stay calm and stick to your plan.

3. **Ignoring Your Plan**
   Breaking your rules destroys consistency. Trust your plan and follow it.

4. **Chasing the Market**
   Jumping into moves out of fear of missing out usually ends badly.

5. **Expecting Quick Results**
   Trading is a marathon, not a sprint. Focus on long-term progress.

Key Takeaway

Avoid bad habits, protect your capital, and stay focused on your long-term goals.

Building Resilience as a Trader

Resilience helps you stay strong during losing streaks, market volatility, and tough times.
It keeps you focused, consistent, and moving forward.

1. Accept that Drawdowns are Normal

Every trader faces losing periods.
Accept them as part of the game, not as failures.

2. Control What You Can

You can't control the market,
but you can control your mindset, plan, and actions.

3. Stay Focused on the Long Term

Don't let short-term results affect your confidence.
Great traders think in years, not in days.

4. Keep a Strong Support System

Surround yourself with positive and like-minded people.
Learn, share, and grow together.

5. Bounce Back and Keep Going

Have setbacks, but don't stay down.
Learn, adjust, and come back stronger.

Key Takeaway

Resilience is what separates good traders from great ones.
Keep going. Your best days are ahead.

Continuous Learning and Adaptation

The markets are always changing.
To stay successful, you must keep learning,
stay flexible, and adapt to new conditions.
Lifelong learning is the key to long-term success.

1. Never Stop Learning

Keep studying the markets, strategies,
and successful traders.
Knowledge is your greatest edge.

2. Adapt to Market Changes

Markets evolve, and so should you.
Adjust your strategies as conditions change.

3. Review and Improve

Review your trades, results, and strategies.
Always look for ways to do better.

4. Stay Open-Minded

Don't get attached to one method or opinion.
Be willing to learn new ideas and perspectives.

5. Grow Every Day

Small daily improvements lead to big results.
Commit to becoming a better trader every day.

The Importance of Risk Management

Risk management is the foundation of long-term success in trading. It's not about avoiding risk, but about controlling it.
Protect your capital, and your capital will protect your future.

1. Protect Your Capital

Your capital is your greatest asset.
Never risk more than you can afford to lose.

2. Use Proper Position Sizing

Risk a small percentage of your capital on each trade.
A common rule is 1% to 2% per trade.

3. Always Use Stop-Losses

A stop-loss protects you from big losses.
Decide your exit before you enter the trade.

4. Maintain a Risk-to-Reward Ratio

Aim for at least a 1:2 risk-to-reward ratio.
Make sure the potential reward is worth the risk.

5. Be Consistent and Disciplined

Follow your risk management rules every time.
Discipline today leads to freedom tomorrow.

Key Takeaway

Good risk management keeps you in the game.
Stay consistent, protect your capital, and success will follow.

The Power of Patience in Trading

Patience is one of the most powerful qualities a trader can have.
The best opportunities take time to develop.
Rushing leads to mistakes, but patience leads to profits.

1. Wait for the Right Setups

Not every market move is a trading opportunity.
Wait for high-probability setups that match your plan.

2. Let the Market Come to You

Don't chase the market.
The best trades come to those who wait.

3. Control Your Impulses

Impulsive trades usually lead to losses.
Stay calm, stay patient, and stick to your plan.

4. Trust Your Plan

Your plan is designed for a reason.
Have patience and let it work.

5. Patience Leads to Consistency

Consistent results come from making smart, patient decisions.
Small wins, over time, create big success.

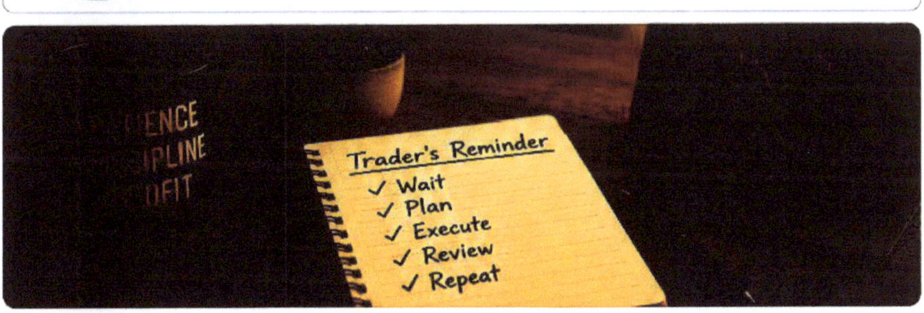

Key Takeaway

Patience helps you make better decisions, avoid costly mistakes, and wait for the trades that truly matter.

The Road to Professional Trading

Becoming a professional trader is a journey, not a shortcut.
It requires the right mindset, skills, discipline, and consistency.
Follow the right path, and success will follow.

1. Build the Right Foundation

Learn the basics, understand the markets,
and master your trading strategy.

2. Develop Your Skills

Practice, backtest, and refine your strategy.
Never stop learning and improving.

3. Create a Trading Plan

Write down your strategy, rules, and risk management.
Your plan is your roadmap to success.

4. Master Risk Management

Protect your capital at all costs.
Consistent risk management leads to long-term growth.

5. Build the Right Mindset

Stay disciplined, patient, and focused.
Control your emotions and trust your plan.

6. Stay Consistent

Consistency beats intensity.
Small, consistent steps lead to big results.

7. Think Long-Term

Focus on becoming a consistently profitable trader.
Long-term success is the ultimate goal.

Key Takeaway

The road to professional trading is built on knowledge,
discipline, patience, and consistency.
Stay committed to the process, and the results will come.

Chapter Summary

Here are the key takeaways from this chapter.

1. Key Insight

Understanding the core concepts is the first step toward becoming a successful trader.

2. Key Lesson

Discipline, patience, and a clear plan are essential for consistent results.

3. Important Strategy

Use the right strategy that aligns with your goals, personality, and market conditions.

4. Risk Management

Protect your capital at all times.
Good risk management is the key to survival.

5. Practice & Improvement

Keep practicing, review your trades, and continuously learn and improve.

Final Thought

Trading is not about quick wins or overnight success.
It is about becoming the best version of yourself.

Stay patient and trust the process.
Great traders are not made in a day.

Focus on progress, not perfection.
Small steps every day lead to big results.

Control your mind, emotions, and actions.
Your mindset is your greatest edge.

Be disciplined, stay consistent, and never stop learning.
The journey is long, but the rewards are endless.

"Success in trading is not about being right all the time, but about managing risk and staying in the game long enough to win."

FINAL CONCLUSION

You have now completed this journey through the world of professional trading.

You have learned the foundations,
developed essential skills, and built a strong mindset.

You have discovered proven strategies and
the importance of risk management.

You have understood that success in trading
comes from discipline, consistency, and patience.

You are now equipped with the knowledge
to take action and create your own path.

Remember, the real learning begins when you start applying what you know.

Believe in yourself. Trust your process.
Stay committed to your goals.
Your future as a successful trader awaits!

Resources

Continue your learning journey with these recommended resources.

Books

Trading in the Zone – Mark Douglas
Market Wizards – Jack D. Schwager
The Intelligent Investor – Benjamin Graham

Websites

Investopedia.com – For trading education
BabyPips.com – For Forex learning
TradingView.com – For charts and analysis

Tools

TradingView – Charting and analysis
MetaTrader 4/5 – Trading platforms
Excel / Google Sheets – For tracking and journaling

Communities

Join trading forums and communities to learn, share, and grow together.

Invest in your knowledge today,
and it will pay you for the rest of your life.

GLOSSARY

Here are the key terms and their meanings used throughout this book.

Asset	Something of value that can be owned and traded, such as stocks, currencies, or commodities.
Bid / Ask	The bid is the highest price a buyer is willing to pay, and the ask is the lowest price a seller is willing to accept.
Candlestick	A type of chart that shows the open, high, low, and close prices of an asset over a specific time period.
Market Trend	The general direction in which the market or an asset is moving (uptrend, downtrend, or sideways).
Risk Management	The process of identifying, assessing, and controlling risk to protect capital.
Stop Loss	An order placed to automatically close a trade at a specific price to limit potential losses.
Trading Strategy	A plan or method used to identify trading opportunities and manage trades effectively.
Volatility	The degree of variation in the price of an asset over time.
Position Size	The amount of capital allocated to a single trade.
Mindset	The mental approach and attitude a trader has toward the markets and trading.

www.ingramcontent.com/pod-product-compliance
Lightning Source LLC
LaVergne TN
LVHW052150210926
848482LV00019B/313
* 9 7 9 8 9 0 5 8 4 8 6 1 2 *